WILLIAMS-SONOMA

MASTERING

Beef & Veal

Author
DENIS KELLY

General Editor
CHUCK WILLIAMS

Photographer
MARK THOMAS

NEW YORK · LONDON · TORONTO · SYDNEY

Contents

About this book

Mastering Beef & Veal offers every reader a cooking class in book form, a one-on-one lesson with a seasoned teacher standing by your side, explaining each recipe step-by-step—with plenty of photographs to illustrate every detail.

Beef and veal play prominent roles in many favorite dishes, so it is important for the home cook to have a thorough understanding of them. After cooking your way through *Mastering Beef & Veal,* you will have learned to make dozens of classic and popular dishes and will have become the kind of confident cook who can prepare nearly every cut of beef and veal a menu demands: a grilled skirt steak, a slowly braised osso buco, a quick stir-fry, or an impressive standing rib roast.

Here's how this book comprises a complete introductory course on beef and veal: The opening pages provide an overview of the most popular cuts along with their preferred cooking methods. You will also find information on selecting quality beef and veal, and on cooking, seasoning, and serving them. The Basic Recipes chapter shows you how to prepare a quartet of homemade stocks and sauces, the building blocks of most braises and of many sauces that accompany beef and veal dishes. You will use these often when making the recipes in subsequent chapters. The Key Techniques chapter teaches you specific cooking skills, from expertly browning meat and deglazing a pan to creating perfect grill marks and checking meat for doneness. Finally, the beef and veal recipes are grouped into four chapters according to how they are cooked: roasted, sautéed & stir-fried, grilled, and braised. Remember, practicing the recipes several times can only increase your skills, ensuring that your dishes are a success every time.

With this book in hand, you are well on your way to mastering the art of cooking beef and veal, a hallmark of the accomplished home cook.

Working with the Recipes

Beef and veal are versatile meats and can be prepared in a variety of ways that fit virtually every occasion, from a simple everyday meal to a formal dinner party. But before you are ready to serve a classic roast beef or osso buco to your family and friends, you need to develop the skills necessary to cook these dishes and then practice them often to build confidence. This book will help you do just that.

This book is organized so that you learn key skills first and then build on them. Each chapter is anchored by at least one master recipe that leads you step-by-step, with words and pictures, through a classic beef or veal recipe. I suggest beginning with these key skill-building recipes. You will find it's like having a cooking teacher alongside you in the kitchen while you work.

Once you have polished the skills you learned in the master recipes, you'll be ready to try some of the other recipes in the chapter, which have only slightly less-detailed text. Many of them are also accompanied by photographs illustrating any confusing or difficult techniques. Continue to practice and your confidence will blossom. Organized like a cooking-class curriculum, this book gives you many opportunities to practice your new skills. For example, once you learn how to make T-Bone Steaks with Black Olive Butter (page 91), you'll have the skills necessary to prepare Veal Chops with Lemon & Sage (page 96) by changing only a few ingredients. You will find variations of recipes throughout the book that will help you further expand your mastery of beef and veal.

Whichever recipe you choose to make, always prepare it when you won't be rushed. Working too quickly can cause mistakes. Also, never make an untried recipe for a dinner party. Practice is the key to success.

To find out more about the basic tools and equipment you will need to make beef and veal, turn to pages 132–35.

Understanding Beef & Veal

Throughout this book, you will learn that if you know what the cut of beef or veal is, and what *primal cut* it comes from, that cut will dictate the best method for cooking it. But before you bring any meat home, you will need to be able to recognize quality at the store. Many factors are important in quality meat, including the color of the flesh, the amount of internal and external fat, and the grade, or quality stamp, on the label.

No matter what the cooking method, the same criteria apply to choosing beef: Look for meat that is bright red with streaks of fat, or *marbling*, running through it. The red indicates that the meat is freshly cut, while the fat in the interior, most of which drains away during cooking, provides juiciness and flavor. Exterior fat should be white to ivory and firm to the touch.

The United States Department of Agriculture (USDA) grades beef on a voluntary basis for meat packers. Marbling is the main way beef is graded and priced in U.S. markets. The more marbling, the more tender, flavorful, and expensive the beef will be. The highest quality—*prime*, or very highly marbled meat—is rarely found in retail markets, since most goes to luxury restaurants. *Choice* meat, well marbled and tender, is available at many quality markets and butchers.

Select meat, with little or no marbling, is the grade most commonly stocked. For the best results, buy USDA choice beef over select meat. Many supermarkets have their own grading system, which can sound suspiciously like USDA grades; ask the butcher or read the label carefully. Officially graded meat will carry the USDA designation.

Range- or grass-fed beef is becoming increasingly available in some markets. I've found it a bit lower in marbling and fat than corn-fed choice beef, but grass-fed steaks are quite tender and have an intense beef flavor.

Veal, meat from young animals, comes in two varieties: milk fed (or formula fed) and grass fed. Milk-fed veal should be pale pink and have visible intra-muscular fat. Its delicate texture and mild flavor is the choice of many consumers. I prefer grass-fed, or "red," veal, which has a more intense flavor and a firmer texture. Choose grass-fed veal that is deep pink. Its fat may have an ivory cast.

Few producers grade their veal (which, as for beef, is voluntary) and prefer instead to use proprietary brand names to indicate quality. Of the graded veal, most prime cuts go to restaurants, while choice and select grades are available to consumers at butcher shops and supermarkets.

Dry-Aged Beef

All beef is aged before selling to improve its flavor and texture. Dry-aged beef has been exposed to air over a period of time to improve tenderness and concentrate flavor. It is not easy to find, but worth the search for its superior taste.

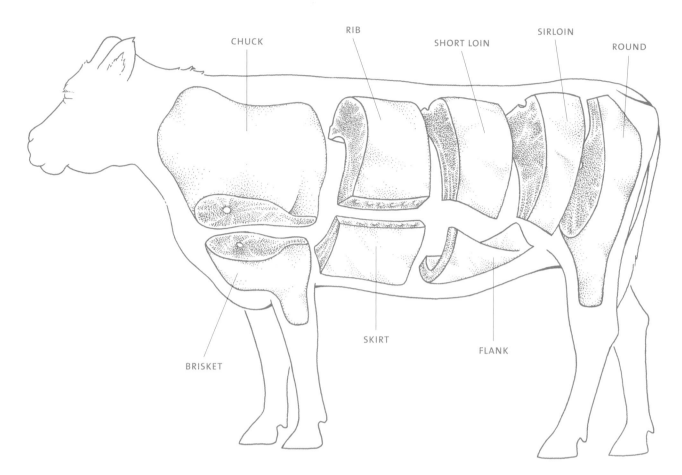

CHUCK   RIB   SHORT LOIN   SIRLOIN   ROUND

BRISKET   SKIRT   FLANK

Cooking Beef & Veal

In cooking school, students learning about beef and veal start with an anatomy class. This is because the cooking methods they will use depend on which part of the animal the meat originated. The general principle is that muscles that get a lot of use, such as the legs, shoulders, hips, and rump, are tougher than muscles along the back, ribs, and loins, which receive less exercise. Each part of the animal requires specific methods of cooking.

In today's marketplace, wholesalers divide beef and veal carcasses into *primal cuts,* or large sections of the animal. If you know which primal cut your piece of meat comes from, you will know which methods are best for cooking it.

Beef is divided into eight primal cuts (working clockwise from the top left of the steer): chuck (or shoulder), rib, short loin, sirloin, round (or rump), flank, skirt (or plate), and brisket (or foreleg). There's some debate over how many primal sections there are for veal, but

for our purposes, it is divided into six sections (working clockwise from the top left of the calf): shoulder, rib, loin, leg, flank, and foreleg/breast.

Beef & Veal for Roasting

Roasting, which is the cooking of meats and other foods in an uncovered pan in the dry heat of an oven, is ideal for beef cuts that are naturally tender and have good marbling. Beef cut from the rib section, such as a standing rib roast; short loin, such as the tenderloin; and

the sirloin, such as a sirloin roast, are perfect candidates. The best veal cuts for roasting come from the loin.

Beef & Veal for Sautéing and Stir-frying

Sautéing and stir-frying both involve cooking relatively small pieces of tender beef or veal over medium-high to high heat for a short period of time. The surface of the meat caramelizes quickly and the interior reaches the rare to medium-rare stage in just a few minutes.

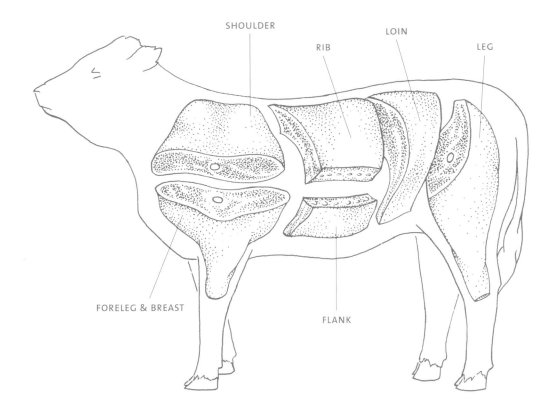

SHOULDER   RIB   LOIN   LEG

FORELEG & BREAST   FLANK

Only tender, little-exercised cuts from the rib or short loin should be used with these quick-cooking techniques.

Small steaks from the tenderloin (a boneless cut from the short loin), such as the filet mignon or medallions, strip steaks from the short loin, and boneless rib-eye steaks from the rib section are all delicious sautéed or pan-seared. Veal medallions and scaloppine cut from the loin can be prepared the same way.

Moderately tender and compact steaks, such as top sirloin and flank steak, are well suited to the Chinese technique of stir-frying. Thinly slicing and marinating the meat make these sometimes chewy cuts even more tender and flavorful.

Beef & Veal for Grilling

Tender steaks and chops that are at least 1½ inches (4 cm) thick are ideal for grilling over a charcoal or gas fire. Porterhouse steaks, T-bone steaks, and filet mignon, all from the short loin, and strip steaks from the sirloin are all excellent grilled or broiled. Chewier steaks, such as flank and skirt, can be grilled successfully, but should be marinated before cooking and cut across the grain to enhance tenderness. And don't forget beef ribs, cut from the rib section, which cook up tender and crisp over the intense heat of a grill. Thick veal rib and loin chops, junior versions of beef T-bone steaks, are also delicious grilled.

Beef & Veal for Braising

Tougher cuts of beef and veal, from the more-exercised parts of the animals, should be slowly cooked in a flavorful and liquid in a covered pot. This breaks down tough muscle tissue.

Beef cuts suitable for braising are from the chuck, brisket, or flank, and the round. Chuck has a higher fat content, ensuring juicier meat. The best veal cuts for the gentle braising process are thick slices from the shank, or leg, and the shoulder, which can be cut into manageable steaks.

Other Cuts of Beef & Veal

To give you a solid foundation of learning, this book teaches only about a select number of meat cuts. As you gain experience with these recipes and want to try your hand at other beef and veal cuts, all you need to remember is that the primal cut dictates the best cooking method.

Measuring Ingredients & Pan Size

An important rule of cooking is to begin by gathering together everything you'll need for the recipe. French-trained chefs call this practice *mise en place*, or "setting in place." In other words, you want to have all the recipe ingredients chopped, if needed, and measured and the equipment required to cook them within easy reach. This prevents you from having to dash around the kitchen looking for ingredients when you should be stirring what's on the stove top.

Basic Ingredient Preparation

Before starting to cook, read over the entire recipe to find out everything you need to complete it. This includes not only ingredients, but also pots, pans, and utensils. If a recipe is cooked in several lengthy stages, note when you'll have time to prepare for the next step. Conversely, for a quick-cooking dish, such as a stir-fry, it is essential to have every element chopped, measured, and ready to go before you begin. Recipes in this book are specific about when to prepare and add the ingredients. Often you'll find you don't need everything in the ingredient list at once.

Begin your *mise en place* by thoroughly rinsing and patting dry all the produce and herbs you will need. Then read the ingredients list again carefully. It alerts you to items that need to be peeled, cut, or diced before measuring.

Choosing the Proper Pan

Choosing the roasting or frying pan is another vital part of your *mise en place*. It is important that you use a pan that fits the amount of meat you will be cooking. Selecting the proper-sized pan critically affects the cooking process: an overly large pan can cause the beef or veal to burn, while a too-small pan can cause the meat to steam, rather than sear.

Get into the habit of measuring your cooking vessels before preparing the beef and veal. This can be done easily and cleanly by first lining your roasting pan, frying pan, or Dutch oven with a piece of parchment (baking) paper that exceeds the length, width, or depth of the pan by a few inches.

Next, place the raw meat in the parchment-lined pan or pot. You will be able to judge immediately whether or not the pan is right for the recipe.

When cooking chops, steaks, or medallions, select a large frying pan in which the meat will fit in a single layer, with about 1 inch (2.5 cm) of space around each piece to allow the air to circulate easily and ensure even cooking and browning.

By the same reasoning, when choosing a roasting pan for a whole tenderloin, a rib roast, or any other sizeable piece of meat, select a pan large enough that it includes 2–3 inches (5–7.5 cm) on the sides of the meat.

You don't want the pan to be too large, however, because as the beef or veal roasts, its juices are drawn out, and in an oversized pan, these juices, or *drippings*, can burn on the bottom of the pan.

Also keep in mind that when you are searing a tenderloin before roasting, it you may need to measure both a frying pan and a roasting pan.

Doneness Temperatures & Food Safety

A handful of everyday habits and some sage cooking practices will safeguard you and your family from the risk of illness from any bacteria present in beef and veal. Keeping raw meat separate from ingredients that will not be cooked and following specific guidelines for doneness are just two of these critical precautions. But perhaps the most important habit to develop is always to work in a clean kitchen with clean tools.

Doneness Temperatures

I recommend cooking beef roasts and steaks to the rare or medium-rare stage to experience the true flavor and texture of the meat. For veal, I recommend cooking to the medium-rare or medium stage. Both beef and veal cooked by moist-heat methods, such as braising, should be cooked until well done. When you become more familiar with cooking these two meats, you'll discover what level of doneness suits your personal taste.

The most reliable way to test most beef and veal for doneness is to use an instant-read thermometer. The chart below offers guidelines on doneness temperatures. As you gain more experience and confidence with your cooking, you will be able to use a visual doneness test, too (page 42).

The Resting Period

Roasts, steaks, and chops that have been cooked with dry heat, such as roasting, grilling, or sautéing, should rest at room temperature for 5–10 minutes before carving or serving. During the resting period, the heat transfers from the surface to the center and the internal temperature of the meat rises 5°–10°F (3°–6°C). This is called *carryover cooking*. During carryover cooking, the juices redistribute themselves evenly, so that when you cut into the meat, the texture is compact and the flavorful juices are not lost. If you don't allow the meat to rest, it can be raw at the center and have an uneven color and texture.

Food Safety

The question of doneness and safety is controversial, prompted in part by cases of poisoning attributed to the presence of *E. coli* bacteria in insufficiently cooked hamburgers. Ground meats have a greater surface area on which bacteria can gather and therefore need to be treated with special precaution. With roasts and steaks, on the other hand, any bacteria on the surface will be killed during cooking. The USDA recommends that all beef be cooked to an internal temperature of at least 140°F (60°C) for safety. Many cooks ignore this recommendation, but if you prefer absolute safety over taste, you should follow the USDA guidelines. One exception: cook all ground beef to the well-done stage (160°F/70°C).

The cardinal rule of food safety is cleanliness. Be sure all your kitchen tools, especially cutting boards that have touched raw meat, are cleaned with hot water and soap after each use. Be particularly careful about cross-contamination—the transfer of bacteria from one food to another—especially between raw meat and poultry and vegetables that will be eaten raw. To avoid this, keep separate cutting boards for meat, poultry, and vegetables, and wash your hands and equipment often.

Always put meat in the refrigerator as soon as possible after purchase until about 1 hour before cooking. Bringing meat to room temperature helps it to cook evenly, though you must keep the time short on hot days.

When using a marinade for basting or as a sauce, take care to prevent cross-contamination. If you want to baste meat with the marinade you do one of two things: either stop basting 5 minutes before the meat finishes cooking, or boil the marinade for 2 minutes before basting with it. Both methods will kill any bacteria present. Similarly, if you want to use the same mixture as both a marinade and a table sauce, set aside enough for the sauce before you marinate. Finally, never return cooked meat to the plate or platter on which it sat when raw.

DONENESS STAGE	TEMPERATURE AFTER COOKING	TEMPERATURE AFTER RESTING
Rare	120°F (49°C)	125°F (52°C)
Medium-Rare	130°F (54°C)	135°F (57°C)
Medium	140°F (60°C)	145°F (63°C)
Medium-Well	150°F (65°C)	155°F (68°C)
Well	160°F (71°C)	165°F (74°C)

Flavoring and Seasoning Beef & Veal

From dry rubs and marinades to the addition of cream or butter to a pan sauce, there are countless ways to flavor beef and veal. Many novice cooks are understandably timid about seasoning, usually afraid that they will add too much of an herb or spice. With time and practice, however, you'll develop a palate for seasonings that reflects your own tastes, and one that your family and friends will appreciate every time they sit at your table.

Flavoring Beef & Veal

I am a firm believer in seasoning beef and veal with salt, pepper, herbs, and spices before cooking. Older cookbooks maintain that salting before cooking draws liquid from the meat and results in a dry, tough dish. Tests have shown, however, that salting and seasoning meat before cooking actually creates a crust that provides great flavor and preserves tenderness and juiciness.

You can simply sprinkle beef and veal with salt and pepper before cooking, or, even better, you can make up an herb or spice rub to coat the surface. The herbs, spices, and salt in the rub react with the meat to make a lightly moist surface that, when browned, mingles with the meat juices to create a savory crust.

I use table salt in my recipes. It mixes well in spice rubs and creates a flavorful crust on the meat. Many chefs favor kosher salt. I advise against using coarse sea salt in most rubs because the grains are too large to mix well with the other ingredients. However, if you like the extra flavor and texture that coarse salt provides, you can sprinkle it on meat just before serving. I do not believe in salting meat heavily, for reasons of both health and taste, so the quantity of salt I use in my recipes is smaller than that used in other cookbooks you might see. Instead of using a lot of salt before cooking the meat, I recommend tasting and adjusting the salt level to your taste just before serving. If you're using purchased stock or broth in a dish, add it judiciously, as even brands labeled "reduced sodium" can be too salty, especially when used in a sauce that is reduced in volume. By the same token, I also prefer reduced-sodium soy sauce. By using it, I can better control the level of seasoning in the finished dish.

My recipes call for freshly ground pepper. I think that the fresher flavor and brighter taste make a big difference, resulting in a sauce or rub with brighter, more intense flavors. It's wise to invest in a top-quality pepper mill that will last for years. Herb and spice rubs, known as dry rubs, are only one way to season beef and veal. Pastes, or wet rubs, can add plenty of flavor, too. To make them, fresh herbs such as thyme, rosemary, and tarragon are finely chopped and then mixed with salt, pepper, garlic, and just enough olive oil to make a thick paste. The herb paste is smeared on the surface of the meat, delivering both flavor and a savory crust.

Marinades are mixtures of oil with acidic or full-flavored liquids, such as wine, citrus juice, beer, soy sauce, or vinegar, and seasonings, such as garlic, onions, and dried or fresh herbs or spices. The meat sits in the liquid for up to an hour at room temperature or for up to 12 hours in the refrigerator. Smaller cuts can gain in flavor and tenderness through marinating, but be careful with tender steaks and chops; do not marinate them for more than an hour or two in acidic marinades, or they will break down too much and develop a mushy texture.

Some marinades and sauces make use of flavorful prepared sauces, many of them Asian. Store-bought sauces made from soy sauce, fermented black beans, chiles, fermented fish, and other pungent ingredients can, if used carefully, add complexity and intense flavor to beef and veal dishes. Experiment and add more or less of a prepared sauce according to your own taste.

The liquid used to braise beef and veal affects the taste and character of the finished dish. My first preference for braising beef is homemade meat stock. You intensify the flavor of the meat by using a matching stock, and if you use a homemade stock, you can control the salt levels more precisely than with purchased stock. However, as a time saver, purchased stock can work well in these recipes. I prefer to use beef or chicken stock in aseptic packages because plastic-coated cartons don't impart the tinny taste sometimes present in canned stocks. You can also purchase excellent "homemade" stocks in fresh or frozen quantities from upscale supermarkets and specialty-foods stores.

I also use wine (red, white, sherry, Madeira, Marsala, port, or vermouth) as a braising liquid and as a base for sauces in many recipes. Red wine imparts a hearty flavor, white wine is subtler and more delicate, and fortified wines, like port or Madeira, contribute nutty and fruity flavors that add complexity and depth. Other liquids, such as vinegar, beer, tomato sauce, citrus and other juices, and soy sauce, all pass on their own particular character.

Developing a Palate for Seasonings

Seasonings such as salt, pepper, herbs, and spices help determine the taste and character of any beef or veal recipe. It is important to remember that the way the dish is flavored before and during cooking contributes to the success of the finished dish just as much as the final seasoning does.

To start developing your own seasoning palate, follow recipes exactly at first, and then add flavors that you like and subtract those that you don't, creating your own versions of each dish.

You might, for example, want to adjust the salt level in some or all of the recipes. Initially follow the recipe as it is written, and then taste the sauce or the piece of meat. If you want more salt, add about ⅛ teaspoon to the sauce or sprinkle the meat lightly with salt. Taste again, and add more salt in small increments if it still tastes bland. If you remember to write down the changes you've made to the dish, the next time you prepare it you'll know how much salt to use.

The key to learning to season is to taste as you cook. I often cut a little bit of meat from a roast or a steak to see how the flavors are developing during cooking. As you grill or sauté a steak, occasionally taste a piece and add more spice rub, salt, or pepper—whatever you think will brighten the flavors. Taste sauces as you cook them down, and adjust the seasonings as you go. And always "finish" the sauce by tasting it and observing the thickness and consistency. A little salt and pepper or a dash of Tabasco can work wonders. If the sauce needs thickening, stir in a *slurry*, a mixture of cornstarch (cornflour) and liquid. If it's too thick, add some stock or wine. If it lacks richness, whisk in butter or cream.

Use the same method for adjusting the quantity of pepper, herbs, and spices, and soon you'll recognize the levels of seasoning you prefer. It's always best to add seasoning in small increments and taste frequently, so that you don't end up overseasoning a dish. Remember to taste a sauce after it has reduced and thickened. Flavors become concentrated as the sauce cooks down.

Other flavor brighteners for beef and veal sauces include lemon or other citrus juices, vinegar (rice vinegar for Asian dishes, red or white wine or balsamic vinegar for many others), chile-based hot sauces such as Tabasco or Asian hot chile oil, soy sauce, Asian fish sauce, and both white and red wines.

Layering Flavors

Here's an example of how I developed the sauce for Beef Medallions with Simple Pan Sauce (page 67). My secret is to taste as I cook and adjust the flavors to my preference. After panfrying the beef medallions in olive oil, I was ready to create the sauce.

I heated a tablespoon of butter in the pan and swirled it to incorporate the pan juices. I wanted the richness of butter in the sauce, since beef medallions cut from the tenderloin, though flavorful, tend to have little fat.

When the butter was frothing up, I stirred in shallots, garlic, and parsley and cooked them for a few minutes. These aromatics, along with the pan juices, formed the basic flavors of my sauce. I chose to use parsley rather than another fresh herb with a more pronounced flavor because I wanted the sauce to have a beefy character.

To deepen the flavors, I stirred 1 cup (8 fl oz/250 ml) meat stock into the pan and reduced it over high heat. I tasted the sauce: nice and beefy with accents of shallots and garlic, but not very lively. I reached for the balsamic vinegar and stirred in a tablespoon. It was good, but not enough. I added another tablespoon and the balance was right: a good hint of tartness and a sweet-sour character underneath the beef flavor.

The sauce seemed a bit thin, though, so I whisked in a tablespoon of tomato paste as a thickener and to add just a hint of sweet tomato to balance the vinegar.

The sauce was almost there, but it needed a little more zip. A teaspoon of Worcestershire sauce brightened the taste nicely. Time to taste for salt. I added just a pinch, since the reduced stock and Worcestershire sauce provided almost enough salt for my taste. I gave the sauce a few grinds of black pepper, stirred, and tasted again. Delicious, but it could use a bit more richness.

I removed the pan from the heat and whisked in ¼ cup (2 fl oz/60 ml) heavy (double) cream. This thickened the sauce a bit and made it velvety smooth and luscious. It was just right.

Serving and Garnishing Beef & Veal

After cooking a beautifully browned roast, steak, or chop or a long-simmered braise, you'll be ready to serve the dish you worked so hard to create. With little additional effort you can add flair—and perhaps some extra flavor—to the presentation. Serving beef and veal often starts with carving or slicing, and then arranging the meat on a platter or individual plates. The finishing touch is a simple, edible garnish.

Many beef and veal cuts are carved or sliced in a manner that further enhances their texture. The main thing one needs to remember is to cut the meat across the grain, or opposite the direction of the muscle fibers. Each recipe includes directions for carving or slicing the meat.

Next, you have some choices for how to present the meat:

FAMILY STYLE This is a casual way of serving beef or veal, in which the meat is brought to the table on the carving board, in its cooking vessel, or on a platter.

Sometimes it is passed at the table for diners to help themselves. Provide a large serving fork or spoon for serving.

RESTAURANT STYLE Here, the food is plated in the kitchen along with any side dishes and a plate is brought to each diner.

Serve the meat on warmed plates or platters. A sprinkle of herbs used in the recipe or a crunchy vegetable cut into small dice, such as a red bell pepper (capsicum), adds flair to the dish. But don't go overboard with your garnishes; the meat should still be the star.

Warming Plates & Platters

To keep your dishes at a pleasing temperature, always serve them on warmed plates or platters. Preheat an oven to 200°F (95°C). Put the plates or platter on the oven rack (make sure they are heatproof) for about 10 minutes to warm. Or, put them on the stove top or near the grill to warm from the ambient heat.

1

Basic Recipes

Learning how to prepare various stocks and sauces is important for mastering a wide repertory of beef and veal dishes. In this chapter, first you'll be taught the steps for making two basic stocks. Then, because tomatoes pair so wonderfully with beef and veal, you'll learn how to cook two different tomato sauces, both of them components of many beef and veal recipes.

Roasted Meat Stock

Roasting the bones and vegetables in a hot oven before simmering them in liquid deepens the overall flavor of the finished stock. When the stock is used in a braising liquid or sauce, this intensity adds a rich, distinctive layer of flavor that enhances the beef or veal.

For the bouquet garni

3 sprigs fresh flat-leaf (Italian) parsley

2 sprigs fresh thyme

4-inch (10-cm) piece celery stalk with leaves

2 bay leaves

Corn oil for preparing the roasting pan

4 lb (2 kg) beef shanks or veal shins, cut into 2-inch (5-cm) pieces by the butcher

2 large yellow onions, unpeeled, quartered

6 large carrots, unpeeled, cut into 2-inch (5-cm) pieces

4 stalks celery, cut into 2-inch (5-cm) pieces

6 cloves garlic, unpeeled, lightly crushed

1½ cups (12 fl oz/375 ml) dry sherry

MAKES ABOUT 4 QT (4 L)

1 **Make the bouquet garni**
If you are not sure how to make a bouquet garni, turn to page 37. Wrap the parsley, thyme, celery, and bay leaves in a piece of damp cheesecloth (muslin) and secure with kitchen string. Set aside.

2 **Brown the shanks and vegetables**
Position an oven rack in the middle of the oven and preheat to 450°F (230°C). Lightly oil a large roasting pan. Spread the beef shank, onions, carrots, celery, and garlic in the pan. Roast, turning the meats and vegetables once or twice, until deep mahogany brown, 20–30 minutes. If the meat and vegetables seem to be browning too fast, reduce the heat to 400°F (200°C).

3 **Deglaze the roasting pan**
For more details on deglazing, turn to page 43. Using a spoon, transfer the meat and vegetables to an 8-qt (8-l), heavy-bottomed pot. Discard any fat in the roasting pan and allow the pan to cool slightly. Place the pan over 2 burners and turn on the heat to medium-high. Carefully, pour the sherry into the pan and, using a wooden spatula, scrape up the dark bits that have cooked onto the bottom of the pan and stir to dissolve them in the sherry. This technique, called *deglazing*, adds a deep caramelized flavor and rich amber color to the finished stock.

4 **Bring the stock to a boil**
Pour the liquid from the pan into the pot holding the browned ingredients. Add the bouquet garni and water just to cover the ingredients by 1 inch (2.5 cm); more water could dilute the flavor of the stock. Place the pot over medium-high heat. Without stirring, slowly bring the liquid to a boil.

5 Simmer the stock

As soon as you see large bubbles begin to form, reduce the heat until only small bubbles occasionally break the surface of the liquid; this is a *simmer*. Use a large spoon to skim the grayish foam that rises to the surface of the liquid for the first 10 minutes of cooking. The foam is the result of collagen and gelatin being released from the bones and meat; if not removed, it will cloud the stock. Simmer the stock uncovered, adjusting the heat periodically to keep the stock at a gentle simmer, for 3–4 hours. Do not stir, but continue to skim the surface as needed, usually every 30 minutes or so. Add more water, if necessary, to keep the ingredients just covered.

6 Strain the stock

Cut a piece of cheesecloth (muslin) large enough to line the inside of a sieve when it is triple layered. Fold the cheesecloth, dampen it with cool water, squeeze it dry, and then use it to line the sieve. Place the sieve over a large tempered-glass or stainless-steel bowl. Remove the larger solids from the stock and then ladle or carefully pour the stock through the sieve. Discard all the solids.

7 Defat or cool the stock

Before you use the stock, carefully remove all of the fat, or the braising liquid or sauce made from it will have a greasy flavor and texture. Use a large metal spoon to skim the clear yellow fat from the surface of the strained stock. Or, if time allows, chill the stock before defatting. Fill a large bowl partway with ice water and set the bowl of stock in the ice bath to cool it to room temperature, stirring occasionally. Cover and refrigerate the stock overnight. The fat will rise to the top and solidify, making it easy to lift off the surface.

8 Store the stock

Cover the cooled stock and refrigerate for up to 3 days, or ladle or pour into airtight containers, filling them to within about ½ inch (12 mm) of the rims (the stock expands as it freezes), and freeze for up to 3 months. To thaw, transfer the frozen stock to a saucepan and melt slowly over low heat, covered, until liquefied. Then, measure the amount needed for the recipes.

CHEF'S TIP

When roasting certain vegetables, such as onion, carrot, and garlic, for stock, many chefs prefer to roast them unpeeled. They believe the peels deepen the flavor of the finished stock.

Chicken Stock

Chicken stock is a staple ingredient in many braising liquids and sauces for veal. Many good stocks and broths are available commercially, but homemade stock has both superior flavor and body. You can make a large batch and then freeze it until you need it.

1 large carrot

1 large or 2 medium yellow onions

1 clove garlic

1 large stalk celery with leaves

6 lb (3 kg) chicken backs and necks

4 sprigs fresh flat-leaf (Italian) parsley

1 bay leaf

8–10 peppercorns

MAKES ABOUT 4 QT (4 L)

1 Chop the vegetables
Peel the carrot, and cut it into 1-inch (2.5 cm) lengths. Then, peel the onion and quarter it through the stem end. Next, peel the garlic, but leave the clove whole. Finally, cut the celery into pieces the same size as the carrot.

2 Bring the stock to a boil
Place the chicken, carrot, onion, garlic, celery, parsley, bay leaf, and peppercorns in an 8-qt (8-l) heavy-bottomed pot and add water just to cover the ingredients by 1 inch (2.5 cm); more water could dilute the flavor of the stock. Place the pot over medium-high heat. Without stirring, slowly bring the liquid to a boil.

3 Simmer the stock
As soon as you see large bubbles begin to form, reduce the heat until only small bubbles occasionally break the surface of the liquid; this is a *simmer*. Use a skimmer or a large slotted spoon to skim the grayish foam that rises to the surface of the liquid for the first 10 minutes of cooking. The foam is the result of collagen and gelatin being released from the bones and meat; if not removed, it will cloud the stock. Simmer the stock uncovered, adjusting the heat periodically to keep the stock at a gentle simmer, for 2–2½ hours. Do not stir, but continue to skim the surface every 30 minutes or so. Add more water, if necessary, to keep the ingredients just covered.

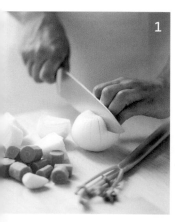   

4 Strain the stock

Cut a piece of cheesecloth (muslin) large enough to line the inside of a sieve when it is triple layered. Fold the cheesecloth, dampen it with cool water, squeeze it dry, and then use it to line the sieve. Place the sieve over a large tempered-glass or stainless-steel bowl. Remove the larger solids from the stock and then ladle or carefully pour the stock through the sieve. Discard all the solids.

5 Defat or cool the stock

Before you use the stock, carefully remove all of the fat, or the braising liquid or sauce made from it will have a greasy flavor and texture. Use a large metal spoon to skim the clear yellow fat from the surface of the strained stock. Or, if time allows, chill the stock before defatting. Fill a large bowl partway with ice water and set the bowl of stock in the ice bath to cool it to room temperature, stirring occasionally. Cover and refrigerate the stock overnight. The fat will rise to the top and solidify, making it easy to lift off the surface.

6 Store the stock

Cover the cooled stock and refrigerate for up to 3 days, or ladle or pour into airtight containers, filling them to within about ½ inch (12 mm) of the rims (the stock expands as it freezes), and freeze for up to 3 months. To thaw frozen stock, refrigerate for 24 hours or transfer the frozen block of stock to a saucepan and melt slowly over low heat, covered, until liquefied. Then, measure the amount needed for the recipes.

CHEF'S TIP

Many chefs prefer to bundle some of the aromatic ingredients in a square of damp cheesecloth (muslin) secured with kitchen string. This bouquet garni (page 37) prevents the ingredients, such as herb sprigs, bay leaves, leafy celery tops, and peppercorns, from floating in the stock and interfering with skimming the surface of impurities.

Basic Tomato Sauce

Keep good-quality canned tomatoes on hand in your pantry to make an easy but tasty tomato sauce for braised beef and veal dishes. I like to infuse the sauce with hearty red wine and spike it with red pepper flakes for a zesty, complex flavor. If you prefer a bolder sauce, use more garlic.

1 yellow onion

3 or 4 cloves garlic

1 tablespoon olive oil

2 tablespoons tomato paste

1 teaspoon dried oregano

1 teaspoon dried thyme

¼ cup (2 fl oz/60 ml) dry red wine such as Zinfandel

1 can (28 oz/875 g) whole tomatoes

1 teaspoon sugar

½ teaspoon red pepper flakes

1 teaspoon salt

⅛ teaspoon freshly ground black pepper

MAKES ABOUT 3 CUPS (24 FL OZ/750 ML)

1 Prepare the onion and garlic

For more details on dicing onions and mincing garlic, turn to pages 32 and 33. Cut the onion in half lengthwise and peel each half. One at a time, place the onion halves, cut side down, on a cutting board. Alternately, make a series of lengthwise cuts, parallel cuts, and then crosswise cuts to create ¼-inch (6-mm) dice. Be sure to stop just short of the root end; this holds the onion together as you cut. Place the garlic cloves on a work surface, firmly press against them with the flat side of a chef's knife, and pull away the papery skin. Use the knife to mince the garlic.

2 Cook the onion and garlic

Place a saucepan over medium heat and add the olive oil. When the oil appears to shimmer, add the onion and cook, stirring often, until translucent, about 5 minutes. Add the garlic and cook until golden, 2–3 minutes longer. Be careful not to burn the garlic, or it will be bitter.

3 Stir in the flavorings

Stir in the tomato paste, oregano, and thyme and cook, stirring often, until the paste is evenly distributed and the onion is a uniform light red, about 3 minutes. The tomato paste, a concentrated form of tomato sauce, enriches and deepens the flavor and color of the the finished sauce.

4 Deglaze the pan

Raise the heat to medium-high, pour in the wine, and stir vigorously with a wooden spoon to scrape up any browned bits that may have cooked onto the bottom of the pan. This technique, called *deglazing*, ensures that all the flavor from the browned vegetables is captured in the sauce. For more details on deglazing, turn to page 43. Cook until the wine is reduced by half, 3–5 minutes. This process of cooking down, or *reducing*, liquid intensifies the flavor of the sauce. To estimate the amount of liquid remaining, tilt the pan occasionally.

5 Simmer the sauce

Add the tomatoes and their juice, the sugar, and the red pepper flakes. The sugar balances the slight acidity in the tomatoes and ensures that the finished sauce has a rounded flavor. Use the wooden spoon to crush the tomatoes slightly. Stirring often, bring the sauce to a boil over medium-high heat. Reduce the heat until only small bubbles occasionally break the surface of the sauce. Simmer, uncovered, until the sauce has a nice spoon-coating consistency, about 10 minutes. During the cooking process, the tomatoes will break down and start to fall apart.

6 Adjust the seasonings

Add the salt and black pepper and stir the sauce for about 3 minutes to distribute the seasonings evenly. Taste the sauce; it should have a bright tomato flavor with a deep background note of wine and accents of herbs and peppers. If it tastes acidic, stir in a pinch more sugar. If it tastes dull, add a little more salt, black pepper, or red pepper flakes until the flavors are nicely balanced.

7 Use or store the sauce

If you are using the sauce right away, measure out the amount you need for the recipe. If you are not using the sauce right away, let it cool to room temperature and then ladle it into 1- or 2-cup (8- or 16–fl oz/250- or 500-ml) containers and refrigerate. It will keep for up to 2 days.

CHEF'S TIP

Italian cooks aren't shy about using canned tomatoes for sauce when fresh tomatoes are not in season, and you shouldn't be either. Look for good-quality canned whole plum (Roma) or other tomatoes. Many Italians reach for canned San Marzano tomatoes, a flavorful variety traditionally grown in southern Italy.

Roasted Tomato Sauce

Roasting tomatoes intensifies their rich, sweet flavor. The same is true of thick onion rounds, whose texture softens and flavor deepens during roasting. Both ingredients are puréed in a food mill to form a bright-tasting summertime sauce accented by a handful of chopped fresh basil.

8 large, ripe tomatoes, about 2 lb (1 kg) total weight

1 large yellow onion

2 tablespoons extra-virgin olive oil

6 cloves garlic

1 tablespoon tomato paste, or more if needed to thicken the sauce

1 large bunch (2 oz/60 g) fresh basil

1 teaspoon salt

1 teaspoon freshly ground pepper

MAKES ABOUT 4 CUPS (32 FL OZ/1 L)

1 Prepare the tomatoes and onion
Preheat the oven to 400°F (200°C). Cut the tomatoes in half crosswise. Next, keeping the onion whole, use a paring knife to peel off the papery skin. Cut a small slice from the side of the onion. This creates a stable surface to make slicing safe and easy. Cut the onion crosswise into rounds ½ inch (12 mm) thick.

2 Roast the tomatoes and onion
Using a pastry brush, coat a large rimmed baking sheet with 1 tablespoon of the oil. Place the tomato halves, cut sides up, and onion rounds on the prepared sheet. Roast, turning often, until the tomatoes bulge slightly and the onion rounds are golden and slightly translucent, 15–20 minutes. Set aside to cool.

3 Prepare the garlic and basil
For more details on chopping garlic and basil, turn to pages 33 and 35. Place the garlic cloves on a work surface, firmly press against them with the flat side of a chef's knife, and pull away the papery skin. Use the knife to mince the garlic. Pick the basil leaves from the stems. Make stacks of 5 or 6 leaves, with the smallest leaves on top. Roll up each stack lengthwise into a tight cylinder and cut crosswise into thin ribbons called *chiffonade*. Measure out ½ cup (¾ oz/20 g).

4 Pass the tomatoes through a food mill, if desired
I like the texture of the tomato skins and seeds in a sauce; however, some cooks prefer to remove them using a food mill. Fit the mill with the large-holed disk and secure the mill over a large bowl. Add the tomatoes to the mill, crushing them slightly with your hand to make them easier to purée. Crank the handle to pass them through the mill into the bowl.

5 Chop the vegetables, if desired

If you did not pass the tomatoes through the food mill, using the tip of a paring knife, make a shallow circular cut in the stem end of the cooled tomatoes to remove the stem. Next, using a chef's knife, chop the tomatoes coarsely. Chop the onion rounds into coarse pieces about the same size as the tomatoes.

6 Simmer the sauce

In a large frying pan over medium-high heat, add the remaining 1 tablespoon oil and the minced garlic. Cook, stirring often, until the garlic is translucent and fragrant, 2–3 minutes. Be careful not to burn the garlic or it will be bitter. Stir in the chopped tomatoes, chopped onion, and tomato paste and cook until the onion further softens, 2–3 minutes. During the cooking process, the tomatoes will break down and start to fall apart. The sauce should have a nice spoon-coating consistency. If the sauce doesn't seem thick enough, stir in additional tomato paste, 1 tablespoon at a time, until you are happy with the consistency.

7 Adjust the seasonings

Stir in the chopped basil, salt, and pepper and stir the sauce for about 2 minutes to distribute the seasonings evenly. Taste the sauce; it should have a bright, pleasantly acidic tomato flavor with a slight sweetness from the roasted onion and a pronounced basil flavor. If it tastes dull, stir in a little more salt and pepper until the flavors are to your liking.

8 Use or store the sauce

If you are using the sauce right away, measure out the amount you need for the recipe. If you are not using the sauce right away, let it cool to room temperature and then ladle it into 1- or 2-cup (8- or 16–fl oz/250- or 500- ml) containers and refrigerate. It will keep for up to 2 days.

CHEF'S TIP

You can also grill the vegetables for this sauce. Grilling the vegetables imparts a nice smoky flavor. Coat whole tomatoes and the onion rounds with 1 tablespoon olive oil and place over a medium-hot fire. Grill, turning once or twice, until they begin to sag, 4–6 minutes. Proceed with the recipe for Roasted Tomato Sauce, starting at step 5.

2

Key Techniques

Mastering the culinary techniques you find in this chapter will make cooking beef and veal—and indeed any recipe— easier. In the pages that follow, you'll find some specific skills, such as how to trim a roast, set up a grill, and test steaks for doneness. You'll also learn some invaluable everyday techniques, including how to dice an onion and deglaze a pan to make a sauce.

Dicing Carrots

1 Trim the carrots
Start with good-quality, unblemished carrots. Use a vegetable peeler to remove the rough skin. Switch to a chef's knife and trim off the leafy tops and rootlike ends.

2 Cut the carrots into lengths
Cut the carrots into even lengths no longer than about 3 inches (7.5 cm). Shorter pieces are simpler to handle, making cutting and then dicing easier.

3 Create a flat surface
Before cutting each length of carrot, cut a thin slice from one side to create a flat surface. Turn the carrot piece onto this flat side to keep it stable while you cut.

4 Cut the lengths into slices
Cut the carrot piece lengthwise into slices as thick as you want the final dice to be. (For example, if you are aiming for ¼-inch/6-mm dice, cut the carrot into ¼-inch slices.)

5 Cut the slices into sticks
Stack 2 or 3 carrot slices and turn them so they are lying on their wide sides. Cut them lengthwise into sticks that are as thick as the first slices.

6 Cut the sticks into dice
Cut the carrot sticks crosswise to create dice. Dicing carrots methodically creates evenly sized pieces that cook at the same rate. Repeat with the remaining carrot lengths.

Dicing Celery

1 Trim the root end
Start with firm, unblemished celery with fresh-looking leaves. Using a chef's knife, trim the head of the celery as needed where the stalks meet the root end. Rinse the stalks.

2 Chop the leaves (optional)
The leaves are used in some dishes to provide extra celery flavor. Cut the leaves from the stalks and chop as directed in a recipe, usually coarsely.

TROUBLESHOOTING
Some celery today is string free, but you may still encounter stringy stalks. The outside ribs may also have a tough outer layer. To remove this layer or any strings, run a vegetable peeler over the stalk.

3 Cut the celery into lengths
Cut the celery stalks into even lengths no longer than about 3 inches (7.5 cm). Shorter pieces are simpler to handle, making slicing and then dicing easier.

4 Cut the lengths into sticks
Cut the celery pieces lengthwise into sticks as thick as you want the final dice to be. (For example, if you are aiming for ¼-inch/6-mm dice, cut the celery into ¼-inch-thick sticks.)

5 Cut the sticks into dice
Cut the celery sticks crosswise to create dice. Dicing celery methodically creates evenly sized pieces that cook at the same rate. Repeat with the remaining celery lengths.

Dicing an Onion or a Shallot

1 Halve the onion or shallot

Using a chef's knife, cut the onion (shown here) or shallot in half lengthwise through the root end. This makes it easier to peel and gives each half a flat side for stability.

2 Peel the onion or shallot

Using a paring knife, pick up the edge of the papery skin at the stem end and pull it away. If the first layer of flesh has rough or papery patches, remove it, too.

3 Trim the onion or shallot

Trim each end neatly, leaving some of the root intact to help hold the onion or shallot half together. Place a half, flat side down and with the root end facing away from you, on the board.

4 Cut the half lengthwise

Hold the half securely on either side. Using a chef's knife, make a series of lengthwise cuts, as thick as you want the final dice to be. Do not cut all the way through the root end.

5 Cut the half horizontally

Spread your fingers across the half to help keep it together. Turn the knife blade parallel to the cutting board and make a series of horizontal cuts as thick as you want the final dice to be.

6 Cut the half crosswise

Still holding the half together with your fingers, cut it crosswise into dice. To mince the pieces, hold the knife tip down with one hand and rock the heel of the knife over them.

Working with Garlic

1 Loosen the garlic peel

Using the flat side of a chef's knife, firmly press against the clove. If you plan to mince the garlic, it's fine to smash it. If you are slicing it, use light pressure to keep the clove intact.

2 Peel and halve the clove

The pressure from the knife will cause the garlic peel to split. Grasp the peel with your fingers, pull it away, and then discard it. Cut the clove in half lengthwise to create flat sides.

TROUBLESHOOTING

You may see a small green sprout running through the middle of the garlic clove, which, if left in, could impart a bitter flavor to the dish. Use the tip of a paring knife to pop out the sprout and discard it.

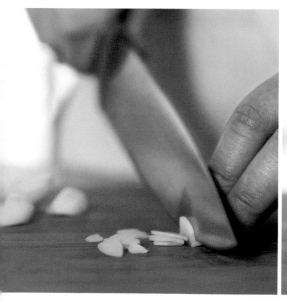

3 Cut the garlic into slices

Working with one clove half at a time, use the knife to cut the garlic into very thin slices. Use the slices, or, if chopping or mincing, gather the slices in a pile in the center of the cutting board.

4 Chop the garlic

Rest the fingertips of one hand on top of the tip of the knife. Move the heel of the knife in a rhythmic up-and-down motion over the garlic slices until coarsely chopped.

5 Mince the garlic

Stop occasionally to clean the knife of garlic bits and gather them in a compact pile on the board. Continue to chop until the garlic pieces are very fine, or *minced*.

Chopping Rosemary

TECHNIQUE

1 Remove the leaves

After rinsing and patting dry the rosemary, remove the leaves by carefully running your thumb and index finger down the woody stem. The leaves resemble pine needles.

2 Chop the rosemary

Using a chef's knife, chop or mince the rosemary leaves. Holding the knife tip with one hand so it stays on the board, rock the knife over the leaves to cut them into small, even pieces.

Chopping Thyme

TECHNIQUE

1 Remove the leaves

After rinsing and patting dry the thyme, remove the leaves by carefully running your thumb and index finger down the woody stem. The leaves resemble small green petals.

2 Chop the thyme

Using a chef's knife, chop or mince the thyme. Holding the knife tip with one hand so it stays on the board, rock the knife over the leaves to cut them into small, even pieces.

Chopping Tarragon

TECHNIQUE

1 Pluck the leaves from the stems

After rinsing and patting dry the tarragon, grasp the leaves between your thumb and index finger and pull them from the stems. The leaves resemble squat blades of grass.

2 Chop the tarragon

Using a chef's knife, chop or mince the tarragon. First, chop the leaves into pieces. Then, holding the knife tip with one hand, rock the knife to cut the leaves into smaller, even pieces.

Chopping Sage

TECHNIQUE

1 Pluck the leaves from the stems

After rinsing and patting dry the sage, grasp the leaves between your thumb and index finger and pull them from the stems. The leaves are gray-green with a soft-looking exterior.

2 Chop the sage

Using a chef's knife, chop or mince the sage. First, chop a stack of leaves into pieces. Then, holding the knife tip with one hand, rock the knife to cut the leaves into smaller, even pieces.

Chopping Parsley

TECHNIQUE

1 Pluck the leaves from the stems

After rinsing and patting dry the parsley, grasp the leaves between your thumb and index finger and pull them from the stems. The leaves have 3 lobes with serrated edges.

2 Chop the parsley

Using a chef's knife, chop or mince the parsley. Holding the knife tip with one hand so it stays on the board, rock the knife rhythmically over the leaves to cut them into small, even pieces.

Chopping Basil

TECHNIQUE

1 Pluck the leaves from the stems

After rinsing and patting dry the basil, pull the leaves from the stems. Stack 5 or 6 leaves on top of one another, preferably of similar size, with the smallest leaves on top.

2 Cut the leaves into thin ribbons

Roll the stack of leaves lengthwise into a tight cylinder. Then, use a chef's knife to cut the leaves crosswise into thin ribbons. These ribbons are known as *chiffonade*.

Grating Lemon Zest

TECHNIQUE

1 Zest the lemon
Lemons are easiest to zest when whole. Use a rasp grater or the small grating holes on a box grater-shredder to remove only the colored portion of the peel, not the bitter white pith.

2 Clean off the grater
Don't forget to scrape all the zest from the back of a grater, where it naturally gathers.

Mincing Lemon Zest

TECHNIQUE

1 Remove the zest
Use a vegetable peeler to remove strips of just the colored portion of the peel, not the bitter white pith. If you mistakenly include some of the pith, scrape it off with a paring knife.

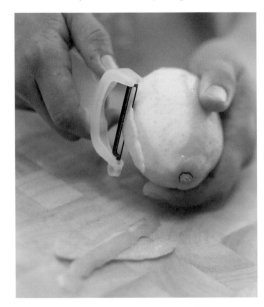

2 Finely mince the zest
Stack 2 or 3 strips together, then use a chef's knife to cut them lengthwise into very thin strips. Cut the strips crosswise into very small pieces.

Peeling & Chopping Fresh Ginger

TECHNIQUE

1 Peel the ginger
Using a vegetable peeler, peel away the papery brown skin to reveal the light, smooth flesh underneath.

2 Chop the ginger
Cut the peeled ginger into disks, and then cut the disks into strips. Cut the strips crosswise to create small pieces. If mincing, rock the knife over the ginger until the pieces are very fine.

TECHNIQUE

Bouquet Garni

1 Wrap the ingredients

Rinse and wring out a 10-inch (25-cm) square of cheesecloth (muslin). Spread the damp cheesecloth out on a work surface and place the ingredients in the middle.

TECHNIQUE

Browning Meat

1 Season the meat

Pat the meat cubes dry with paper towels. This helps them brown properly. Put the meat in a large glass bowl and season it, rubbing the pieces to coat them evenly.

2 Add the beef to the pan

Place a large, heavy pan over medium-high heat. When it's hot, add the oil and wait until surface of the oil shimmers, or wavers. Then use tongs to add the seasoned meat to the pan.

2 Tie the bundle

Bring the corners of the cheesecloth together and tie them with an 8-inch (20-cm) length of kitchen string, forming a secure bundle.

3 Cook until dark golden brown

Cook as directed in the recipe, using tongs to turn the meat to brown the other surfaces. The meat should be a dark golden brown with a crisp and slightly caramelized exterior.

TROUBLESHOOTING

A crowded pan will cause the meat to steam, rather than brown. To prevent this from happening, brown the meat in batches, removing each batch as it is ready.

Trimming a Roast

1 Trim the fat from the roast
Using a rigid boning knife or a chef's knife, begin to cut away the external fat on the surface of the roast. Cut the fat off in long, uniform strips to ensure an even layer.

2 Leave some fat on the roast
Leave a layer of fat ¼–½ inch (6–12 mm) thick on the roast. This small amount will help to flavor and moisturize the meat as it cooks. Discard the fat you removed.

Trimming a Steak

1 Trim the fat
Using a rigid boning knife or a chef's knife, trim away most of the external fat around the edge of the steak. For rib-eye steaks, also cut out the nugget of fat that's often found in the center.

TROUBLESHOOTING
Steaks can curl when cooked over high heat. To prevent this from happening, use a rigid boning knife or a paring knife to *score* the steaks: Cut 2 or 3 shallow, evenly spaced slashes in the surrounding fat.

2 Leave on a thin layer of fat
Leave a layer of fat ¼–½ inch (6–12 mm) thick on the steak. This small amount will help to flavor and moisturize the meat as it cooks. Discard the fat you removed.

3 Put the steaks on a plate
As you trim the steaks, put them on a plate in a single layer. If you stack them on top of each other, they will pull juices from one another.

Trimming a Beef Tenderloin or Filet Mignon

1 Trim off the tenderloin tail
Place the meat on a cutting board, and notice the thin end of the fillet; this is called the *tail*. Using a chef's knife or rigid boning knife, cut off the tail and reserve it for another use.

2 Begin to remove the fat
With the boning knife or chef's knife, use long, even strokes to remove the fat from the exterior of the tenderloin. Try not to tear the meat as you trim.

3 Ensure all the fat is removed
As you work, turn the tenderloin on the board and continue to remove the fat in sections. You want the tenderloin to be completely free of external fat.

4 Locate the silver skin
Look for the thin, white membrane, called *silver skin*, running the length of the meat; it is very tough. Slide the knife under the silver skin to free the tip of the silver skin from the flesh.

5 Pull the silver skin taut
Position the knife where the silver skin meets the flesh and begin to cut, using your fingers to pull the silver skin in the direction of the cut. Angle the knife against the skin, not the meat.

6 Remove the silver skin
As you work, turn the tenderloin and continue to remove the silver skin in sections. Do not pull too hard or work too fast or you might tear off some of the meat with the silver skin.

Direct-Heat Charcoal Grilling

1 Add the ignited coals to the grill
Ignite the coals using a chimney starter (follow the manufacturer's directions). Pour the lit coals into the fire bed along with enough additional coals to cover the fire bed fully.

2 Arrange the coals
Using long tongs, arrange the coals 2 or 3 layers deep in one-third of the fire bed and 1 or 2 layers deep in another one-third of the fire bed. Leave the last third of the fire bed free of coals.

Indirect-Heat Charcoal Grilling

1 Arrange the coals
Ignite the coals and arrange in 2 equal piles on 2 sides of the grill, leaving a space in the center free of coals.

3 Replace the grate on the grill
Position the grill grate in its slots over the coals. Let the coals burn until the desired heat level is reached.

4 Check the heat level of the grill
Hold your hand over the highest level of coals to test the heat level. If you can count to 4 before pulling your hand away, the grill is at medium-high heat.

2 Position a drip pan
Place a drip pan, such as a disposable aluminum foil pan, in the space between the coals to catch dripping fat or juices. Position the grill grate in its slots over the coals.

Setting Up a Gas Grill

1 Attach the propane tank
Open the grill lid and make sure the burners are off, then check the propane tank to ensure it has fuel. Follow the manufacturer's directions to connect the fuel source to the grill.

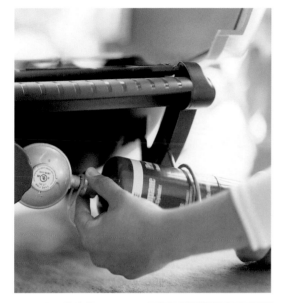

2 Ignite the grill
Follow the manufacturer's directions to ignite the gas grill. Adjust the heat to the desired level and let the grill heat for about 15 minutes before cooking on it.

Creating Crosshatch Grill Marks

1 Line up the steaks
Place the steaks on the grill, making sure they all face the same direction. Remember the order you put them on the grill, so you know which one to turn first.

2 Rotate the steaks
Leave the steaks undisturbed for 1–1½ minutes to develop good grill marks. Using tongs, rotate each steak 90 degrees and continue cooking undisturbed for 1–1½ minutes.

3 Turn over the steaks
Starting with the first steak, turn the steaks over, again lining them up in the same direction. You'll notice the square shaped crosshatching you created by rotating the steaks.

4 Crosshatch the second side
Leave the steaks undisturbed for 1–1½ minutes to develop good grill marks. Using tongs, again rotate each steak 90 degrees and continue cooking for 1–1½ minutes.

Testing Doneness by Temperature

1 Testing a steak for doneness
Insert an instant-read thermometer into the thickest part of the meat away from the bone.

Testing Doneness Visually

1 Cut into the meat
Use a paring knife to make a small cut in the thickest part near the center of the meat (away from the bone, if present). Pull the meat apart and note its color.

2 Rare meat
Beef cooked to the rare stage is deep red at the center and very juicy. It is not recommended to cook and serve veal rare.

2 Testing a roast for doneness
Insert an instant-read thermometer into the center of the roast away from the bone. Remember, the temperature will rise 5°–10°F (3°–6°C) as it rests. For accuracy, test in 2 different places.

3 Medium-rare meat
Beef cooked to the medium-rare stage is deep pink in the center. It will be firmer than rare beef but still juicy. Medium-rare veal is pink at the center.

4 Medium meat
Beef cooked to the medium stage will be light pink in the center. The texture is firm and compact. Medium veal is also light pink at the center.

Carving Roasts

1 Slice the meat

Without inserting the tines too deeply, use a fork to hold the roast steady. Using a carving knife or chef's knife, cut the meat across the grain into slices ¼–½ inch (6–12 mm) thick.

Deglazing

1 Add liquid to a hot pan

Place a pan containing the browned drippings left by cooking beef or veal—called the *fond*—over medium-high heat until the drippings sizzle. Add stock or another liquid.

Using a Slurry

1 Stir the ingredients together

Using a fork, stir together the cornstarch (cornflour) and a cold liquid until completely blended. The mixture should be the consistency of heavy (double) cream.

2 Transfer the slices to a platter

Grasp 1 or more slices of meat between the knife and fork and carefully transfer them to a warmed platter. Tent the platter with aluminum foil to keep the meat warm.

2 Scrape up the browned bits

As the liquid comes to a boil, stir and scrape the bottom and sides of the pan with a wooden spatula to loosen the brown *fond*. It will be absorbed into the liquid for flavor and color.

2 Whisk the mixture

Whisk the slurry into simmering or boiling liquid to activate its thickening power. If needed, whisk in more slurry a little at a time and cook until thickened as desired.

3

Roasted
Beef & Veal

In this chapter, you will learn about roasting, the oldest and one of the most popular ways to cook beef and veal. Whether you choose a beef tenderloin wrapped in a savory salt crust, a standing rib roast accompanied by Yorkshire pudding, or an herb-rubbed veal loin, roasting these tender cuts in the dry heat of an oven yields juicy, flavorful interiors and rich, caramelized exteriors.

Prime Rib with Individual Yorkshire Puddings

I like to coat this large, tender cut from the rib section with a paste of garlic and fresh herbs, which roasts to a beautiful browned, flavorful crust. My version also includes single-serving-sized Yorkshire puddings, puffy, golden brown popovers flavored with the pan drippings that I bake in muffin cups.

1 Prepare the meat

If you need help trimming the meat, turn to page 38. Using a rigid boning knife or a chef's knife, trim all but ¼–½ inch (6–12 mm) of fat from the exterior of the meat. Resist the urge to remove all of the the fat; it keeps the meat moist during cooking and adds flavor. Use the tip of the knife to cut through the fat layer in 4 or 5 places across the top of the meat, making slits about ⅛ inch (3 mm) wide and ½ inch (12 mm) deep. These will form little pockets into which the garlic-herb paste can sink and flavor the meat from the inside.

2 Make the garlic-herb paste

For more details on mincing garlic and herbs, turn to pages 33 and 34. Place the garlic cloves on a work surface, firmly press against them with the flat side of a chef's knife, and pull away the papery skin. Rock the knife rhythmically over the garlic to mince it. Next, pull the thyme and rosemary leaves from the stems and discard the stems. Rock the knife rhythmically over the herbs to mince them. In a small bowl, combine the minced garlic, thyme, rosemary, salt, and pepper. With a wooden spoon, stir in the 1 tablespoon olive oil. You are aiming for a thick paste that can be easily smeared over the meat. If it does not look like this, stir in a little more olive oil until it looks and feels right.

3 Coat the meat with the paste

Using your fingers, spread the paste over the fat layer of the meat, coating it evenly and pushing some of the paste into the slits. Lightly cover the coated meat with plastic wrap and let stand for at least 30 minutes and up to 1 hour so that the meat has time to absorb the flavors from the paste and to encourage even roasting.

4 Preheat the oven

At least 15 minutes before you plan to start cooking, position an oven rack in the middle of the oven. This will guarantee even cooking and browning from all sides. Turn your oven to 450°F (230°C). This is a high temperature, but you need the intense heat to produce a browned, tasty crust. The temperature is reduced later to ensure that the meat cooks through and is juicy. ▶

1 standing rib roast, chine bone (see page 51) removed by the butcher, 6–8 lb (3–4 kg)

For the paste

8 cloves garlic

10 sprigs fresh thyme

5 sprigs fresh rosemary

1 tablespoon salt

1½ teaspoons freshly ground pepper

1 tablespoon olive oil, plus extra if needed for thinning

For the Yorkshire puddings

1 cup (8 fl oz/250 ml) whole milk

3 large eggs

1 teaspoon salt

1 cup (5 oz/155 g) all-purpose (plain) flour

2 tablespoons pan drippings from roast or melted vegetable shortening (vegetable lard)

1 cup (8 fl oz/250 ml) Roasted Meat Stock (page 20)

1 teaspoon salt

½ teaspoon freshly ground pepper

MAKES 12 SERVINGS

CHEF'S TIP
For the best-quality rib roast, ask the butcher for the "first cut," which comes from the loin end of the steer and has the biggest eye.

5 Make the Yorkshire pudding batter

While the oven preheats, you'll have time to make the batter for the Yorkshire puddings. In a blender container, combine the milk, eggs, and salt and process until the mixture is smooth. With the blender running, gradually add the flour through the opening in the lid and process until it is completely incorporated and the mixture looks like thin pancake batter. Let the batter stand, in the covered blender, at room temperature for at least 1½ hours while the roast cooks. Room-temperature batter bakes up into light, airy puddings. If the batter must sit for more than 2 hours, refrigerate it, but bring it to room temperature, about 30 minutes, before baking.

6 Choose a roasting pan

Choose a heavy-gauge roasting pan and a roasting rack that fits snugly in the pan. You don't want the rack to slide around when the pan is moved. Position the meat, with the bones down, on the rack. Roasting the meat on a rack allows the hot air to circulate around the meat and helps to brown the surface, while the drippings fall into the pan below.

7 Roast the beef

Turn on your oven ventilation or open a window and put the pan with the meat in the oven. In 10–15 minutes, open the oven and check the roast. The garlic-and-herb paste should have formed a golden-brown crust. You may also notice a small amount of smoke coming out of the oven, which will cease as soon as the oven heat is reduced. If the crust hasn't yet turned golden brown, let the meat roast for a few more minutes. When the crust has browned, reduce the heat to 350°F (180°C). Reducing the heat helps the meat stay moist and prevents excessive shrinkage, which can happen at high temperatures.

8 Test the meat for doneness

Place a platter on the stove top to warm from the heat of the oven. To find out more about checking meat for doneness, turn to page 42. Although the total roasting time is 1½–2 hours, it can vary, depending on the weight and shape of the meat. Start checking early to prevent overdone meat. After 1½ hours of total roasting time, insert an instant-read thermometer into the center of the meat, away from the bone. If you like your beef rare, it should register 120°F (49°C). For medium-rare, wait until it registers 130°F (54°C). If the meat isn't ready, continue to roast it for 15 minutes longer, then check again. The internal temperature will rise 5°–10°F (3°–6°C) after the meat is removed from the oven.

9 Let the meat rest

When the meat is done, transfer it to the warmed platter. Loosely cover the roast with aluminum foil and let rest for 15–20 minutes. This resting period gives the juices, which rise to the surface during cooking, an opportunity to settle and redistribute themselves throughout the roast. The meat also firms up while it rests, which makes carving easier.

10 Bake the Yorkshire puddings

While the meat is resting, bake the Yorkshire puddings. Raise the oven temperature to 450°F (230°C) and put a heavy-gauge, 12-cup muffin pan on a work surface. Using a bulb baster or spoon, carefully remove about 2 tablespoons of the fat from the roasting pan and divide the fat among the muffin cups (don't worry if the measurements aren't exact). Place the muffin pan in the hot oven. When the fat is very hot and starts to smoke, after 5–7 minutes, carefully remove the pan from the oven. It is important that both the pan and the fat be very hot when you pour in the batter; this immediately cooks the batter as it comes into contact with the pan and helps the puddings puff. Pour the batter into the muffin cups, filling them half full. Bake for 15 minutes. The puddings will puff up about 2 or 3 inches (5 or 7.5 cm) above the rim of the pan. Turn off the oven. Leave the puddings in the oven to dry out for 10 more minutes. Resist the urge to open the oven door during this time, or the puddings will collapse.

11 Defat the pan juices

Much of the flavor from the meat is still in the pan drippings, so I like to defat them and then use the pan juices as a sauce for the meat. Pour the stock into the roasting pan and, using a wooden spoon, stir it into the drippings from the meat. Put the pan in a cool spot for 10–15 minutes. The fat will rise to the surface of the juices for easier skimming. Use a large metal spoon to skim the fat from the surface. To remove any potentially burned pieces of garlic from the sauce, strain it through a medium-mesh sieve into a bowl and pour it into a small saucepan.

12 Carve the meat

Place a serving platter and a small bowl or sauceboat on the stove top to warm from the heat of the oven. Carve the meat (see opposite page) and arrange the slices on the warmed platter. Cover them with aluminum foil to keep warm.

13 Warm the meat juices and adjust the seasonings

Pour the meat juices from the carving board and original platter into the saucepan with the other juices. Place the saucepan over medium-high heat and bring to a boil. As soon as you see bubbles begin to form, reduce the heat to low and let it bubble slowly for 2–3 minutes. Add the salt and pepper and taste the juices. They should taste rich and meaty, with accents of garlic, thyme, and rosemary. If the juices taste dull, stir in a little more salt and pepper until the flavor is to your liking. Pour the sauce into the warmed bowl.

14 Serve the meat and Yorkshire puddings

Remove the muffin pan from the oven and, using the tip of a paring knife, lift out each pudding. Arrange the puddings on a plate or in a basket and pass them with the platter of sliced meat and the sauce at the table. The puddings will quickly deflate, so serve them as soon as possible after they come out of the oven (they still taste good even when they are a little flat).

Carving a standing rib roast

A standing rib roast can be intimidating to novice carvers. However, if you ask the butcher to remove the chine bone (part of the animal's backbone) from any rib roast, carving is much easier. The basic tools to have on hand are a stable carving board with grooves to capture the meat juices, a long meat fork, and a sharp carving knife that feels comfortable in your hand.

Remove the bones from the roast (top left)

Use a carving fork and tongs to transfer the roast, with the bones upright, to a carving board. Using the tines of the fork to brace the roast and a long, sharp carving knife, cut the rib bones away from the large, meaty section, which is called the *eye*.

Cut the roast into slices (left)

Turn so the crust faces up. Cut the meat across the grain (or opposite the direction of the muscle fibers) into slices ¼–½ inch (6–12 mm) thick.

Separate the bones (above)

If your guests enjoy the flavorful meat attached to the bones, cut between the ribs to separate them and offer them to diners.

Salt-Roasted Tenderloin

Roasting beef tenderloin—the prized roast from the short loin section—in a salt crust makes a dramatic presentation and results in succulent meat that is, surprisingly, not overly salty. The herb-flecked dough encases the meat, sealing in its natural flavor and juices as it roasts. The crust is cut away before serving.

1 Separate the eggs

Put 2 small bowls side by side on the work surface. To avoid stray shell bits, crack the egg sharply on its side on a flat surface rather than the rim of a bowl. Holding the egg over one of the bowls, carefully pull the shell halves apart. Transfer the yolk back and forth between the halves, allowing the white to drop into the bowl. Put the yolk into the second bowl. Repeat with the remaining egg. For this recipe you'll be using only the whites, which help the crust adhere to the meat. Cover the yolks with plastic wrap and save them for another use, such as the béarnaise sauce on page 62.

2 Make the salt-crust dough

In a large bowl, combine the salt, flour, sage, thyme, water, and egg whites; then, with clean hands, mix the ingredients until they are evenly blended. Keep mixing, folding, and pressing the dough in the bowl several times until it feels moist and sandy, 3–4 minutes. The salt will give it a slightly rough texture. Keep the dough in the bowl and cover the bowl with plastic wrap. Refrigerate for at least 3 hours or up to overnight. The resting period makes the dough easier to handle and shape.

3 Trim the meat

If you are not sure how to trim a tenderloin, turn to page 39. Put the meat on a cutting board and find the thin end of the tenderloin; this is called the *tail*. Using a rigid boning knife or a chef's knife, trim off the tail and reserve it for another use. You should now have a piece of meat 10–12 inches (25–30 cm) long. Using the same knife, trim all the fat from the exterior of the meat. Notice the thin white membrane on the outside of the meat; this is called the *silver skin*. Slide a thin knife, preferably a boning knife, under the silver skin at one end of the tenderloin. Keeping the knife pointed slightly upward while pulling the silver skin taut with your other hand, cut along the silver skin to separate it from the meat.

For the salt crust

2 large eggs

2 cups (1 lb/500 g) kosher salt

2¼ cups (11 oz/345 g) all-purpose (plain) flour, plus extra for dusting

1 cup (8 fl oz/250 ml) water

1 tablespoon minced fresh sage (page 35)

1 tablespoon minced fresh thyme (page 34)

1 whole beef tenderloin, 6½–7 lb (3.25–3.5 kg)

2 teaspoons freshly ground pepper

2 tablespoons olive oil, plus extra for preparing the pan

MAKES 8–10 SERVINGS

CHEF'S TIP
The excess meat left over after trimming the tail from the beef tenderloin can be sliced thinly and used in other recipes, such as in stir-fries.

4 Season the meat

Sprinkle the meat with the pepper, pressing the pepper into the meat with your fingertips. (You won't need to use salt here, as the crust has more than enough.) Let the meat stand for at least 30 minutes and up to 1 hour at room temperature to encourage even cooking and let the pepper permeate the meat.

5 Preheat the oven and prepare the pan

At least 15 minutes before you plan to start cooking, position a rack in the middle of the oven (this will ensure even cooking and browning) and preheat the oven to 400°F (200°C). Lightly oil a rimmed baking sheet and set it aside.

6 Brown the meat

Select a large frying pan in which the tenderloin fits nicely from end to end, without being crowded. A pan about 12 inches (30 cm) in diameter is about right. Put the pan on the stove over high heat. When it feels hot (you'll be able to feel the heat rising upward when you hold your hand over the pan), add the 2 tablespoons olive oil and heat until the surface appears to shimmer. Put the meat in the pan and let it cook, undisturbed, until the part touching the pan is golden brown, 2–3 minutes. Using tongs, turn the meat and repeat the browning process until the whole surface of the tenderloin is browned. Browning, or *searing,* meat in this way caramelizes its surface, which results in richer and more complex flavor. Using the tongs, transfer the meat to a platter while you roll out the crust.

7 Roll out the salt-crust dough

Generously dust a work surface with flour. Remove the dough from the refrigerator and transfer it to the middle of the floured work surface. Using a well-floured rolling pin, roll the dough in all directions, using even, steady pressure, into a rectangle ¼ inch (6 mm) thick and 4 inches (10 cm) wider and 6 inches (15 cm) longer than the roast. If necessary, trim it to fit these dimensions and reserve any dough scraps. If the dough starts to stick to the work surface or rolling pin, sprinkle them with additional flour. >

CHEF'S TIP

Tenderloins are sold "peeled" and "unpeeled." Peeled tenderloins, what you usually find in the meat case, typically have only small, thin patches of exterior fat, while unpeeled tenderloins have a thick layer of fat that must be trimmed away before cooking.

8 Wrap the meat in the salt crust and roast it

When the tenderloin is cool to the touch, place it lengthwise on one long edge of the dough. Lightly dust your hands with flour, then roll the dough around the meat until it is halfway encased in the dough. Fold each end of the dough inward to enclose the ends of the meat. Finish rolling the meat in the dough until it is completely wrapped; it will look like a large spring roll. Seal any gaps in the dough with bits of extra dough. The meat needs to be completely encased in the dough to seal in the flavorful juices. Place the enclosed meat, seam side down, on the prepared baking sheet and put it in the oven.

CHEF'S TIP

When cooking meats in an enclosed environment, such as a salt crust, carryover cooking (page 13) will be a larger factor and cause the postcooking temperature to rise more than usual. To compensate for this difference, you need to remove such roasts from the oven at a lower internal temperature than usual (about 5°F/3°C lower).

9 Test the meat for doneness

Place a serving platter on the stove top to warm from the heat of the oven. To find out more about checking meat for doneness, turn to page 42. Although the total roasting time is 30–40 minutes, depending on the weight and shape of the meat, start checking early to prevent overdone meat. After 20 minutes of roasting time, insert an instant-read thermometer through the crust into the center of the meat. If you like your beef rare, it should register 115°F (46°C). For medium-rare, wait until it registers 120°F (49°C). If the meat isn't ready, continue to roast for 10 minutes longer, then check again. The internal temperature will rise 10°–15°F (6°–8°C) after the roast is removed from the oven. When the tenderloin is done to your liking, remove it from oven and let it rest on a carving board for about 25 minutes. This gives the juices, which rise to the surface during cooking, an opportunity to settle and redistribute themselves throughout the meat. The beef also firms up while it rests, which makes carving easier.

10 Serve the meat

Using tongs, carefully transfer the roast to the warmed platter and present the roast to guests. Using a chef's knife or a carving knife, cut away the salt crust and discard. Use the same knife to slice the tenderloin into steaks 1 inch (2.5 cm) thick and serve on individual plates.

Serving ideas

A whole roasted beef tenderloin is a delicious and dramatic centerpiece for an elegant dinner. After presenting the tenderloin in its salt crust to your guests, you have a few choices for serving it. You can cut it into thick steaks and top with a horseradish cream sauce, or you can slice it thinly for a main-course salad. Yet another idea is to serve 3 or 4 thin steaks with a side of tender-crisp vegetables.

Tenderloin steaks with horseradish (top left)
Stir together 2 cups (1 lb/500 g) sour cream, 3–4 tablespoons prepared horseradish, ¼ teaspoon salt, and ¼ teaspoon freshly ground pepper. Top each steak with a dollop of the horseradish sauce.

Steak salad (left)
Using a chef's knife, cut the tenderloin into thin slices. Serve with mixed greens, crumbled blue cheese, and your favorite vinaigrette.

Sliced steaks with green beans (above)
Beef cooked this way is flavorful enough to serve on its own. Cut the tenderloin into slices ¼ inch (6 mm) thick and accompany the small steaks with steamed green beans.

Classic Roast Beef with Root Vegetables

A tradition in many American households is the Sunday "roast," a gorgeously browned piece of tender beef surrounded by golden brown potatoes and root vegetables. To give it a modern spin, I like to season the beef with a paste of fresh herbs and garlic, which becomes a flavorful, attractive crust during roasting.

1 boneless sirloin roast, rib-eye roast, or strip loin roast, 4–5 lb (2–2.5 kg)

For the paste

4 cloves garlic, minced (page 33)

1 tablespoon minced fresh thyme (page 34)

2 teaspoons salt

1 teaspoon freshly ground pepper

1 tablespoon olive oil, plus extra for thinning

6 Yukon gold potatoes, scrubbed and quartered

3 turnips, peeled and quartered

3 carrots, peeled and cut into 1-inch (2.5-cm) pieces

3 parsnips, peeled and cut into 1-inch (2.5-cm) pieces

1 tablespoon extra-virgin olive oil

2 teaspoons minced fresh rosemary (page 34)

1 teaspoon salt

½ teaspoon freshly ground pepper

MAKES 6–8 SERVINGS

CHEF'S TIP
Don't worry if the vegetables aren't quite ready at the same time as the meat. You can continue to roast them while the meat rests.

1 **Prepare the meat**
If you need help trimming the meat, turn to page 38. Trim all but ¼–½ inch (6–12 mm) of fat from the exterior of the meat. Use the tip of the knife to cut through the fat layer in 4 or 5 places across the top of the meat, making slits about ⅛ inch (3 mm) wide and ½ inch (12 mm) deep. Put the meat on a plate.

2 **Coat the meat with the garlic-thyme paste**
In a small bowl, combine the garlic, thyme, salt, and pepper. Stir in the 1 tablespoon olive oil. If needed, stir in a little more oil until the mixture looks and feels like a thick paste. Using your fingers, spread the paste evenly over the meat, pushing some of the paste into the slits on top. Let the meat stand at room temperature for 30–60 minutes before roasting.

3 **Preheat the oven and season the vegetables**
At least 15 minutes before you start cooking, position a rack in the middle of the oven and preheat to 350°F (180°C). In a large bowl, using 2 large spoons, toss the potatoes, turnips, carrots, and parsnips with the extra-virgin olive oil and rosemary. Sprinkle them with the salt and pepper and toss again.

4 **Roast the meat and vegetables**
Put the meat in a heavy-gauge roasting pan. It should fit with about 3 inches (7.5 cm) of space around it for the vegetables. Roast the meat for 30 minutes, then add the vegetables to the roasting pan. Continue to roast the meat and vegetables, using a spoon or tongs to turn the vegetables about every 30 minutes so they brown evenly. Although total roasting time should be 1–1½ hours, depending on the weight and shape of the meat, start checking early to prevent overdone meat. After 45 minutes total, insert an instant-read thermometer into the center of the meat; it should register 120°F (49°C) for rare or 130°F (54°C) for medium-rare. If the meat isn't ready, continue to roast for 10–15 minutes longer, and check again. Insert the tip of a knife into the vegetables; it should slip in easily. To find out more about checking meat for doneness, turn to page 42.

5 **Let the meat rest, then carve and serve**
When the meat is done, transfer it to a carving board. Loosely cover it with aluminum foil and let rest for 10–20 minutes. Place individual plates on the stove top to warm from the heat of the oven. Keep the vegetables warm by covering the pan with aluminum foil. Use a carving knife and carving fork to slice the roast thinly across the grain. For more details on carving roasts, turn to page 43. Serve the sliced meat with the roasted vegetables on the warmed plates.

Herb-Rubbed Veal Loin

This tender, lean cut of veal is kept moist by an herb rub that coats the surface and forms a flavorful golden-brown crust as the meat roasts. When the veal is sliced, you will see where the tarragon and garlic have worked their way under the surface of the meat, forming small pockets of color and flavor, which then mingle with the veal's natural juices.

1 Trim the meat
If you need help trimming the meat, turn to page 38. Trim all but ¼–½ inch (6–12 mm) of fat from the exterior of the meat. Use the tip of the knife to cut through the fat layer in 4 or 5 places across the top of the meat, making slits about ⅛ inch (3 mm) wide and ½ inch (12 mm) deep. Put the meat on a plate.

2 Coat the meat with the garlic-tarragon paste
In a small bowl, combine the garlic, tarragon, salt, and lemon pepper. Stir in the 1 tablespoon olive oil. If needed, stir in a little more olive oil until the mixture looks and feels like a thick paste. Using your fingers, spread the paste evenly over the meat, pushing some of the paste into the slits on top. Let the meat stand at room temperature for 30–60 minutes before roasting.

3 Roast the veal
At least 15 minutes before you plan to start cooking, position an oven rack in the middle of the oven and preheat to 350°F (180°C). Choose a heavy-gauge roasting pan and a roasting rack that fits snugly in it. You don't want the rack to slide around when the pan is moved. Put the veal on the rack and put the pan in the oven. Although the total roasting time is 1½–2 hours, it can vary depending on the weight and shape of the meat. Start checking early to prevent overdone meat. After 1 hour, insert an instant-read thermometer into the center of the meat, away from the bone if there is one. It should read 130°F (54°C) for medium-rare (pink at the center) or 140°F (60°C) for medium (light pink at the center). If the meat isn't ready, continue to roast for 15 minutes longer, and check again. To find out more about checking meat for doneness, turn to page 42.

4 Let the meat rest, then carve and serve
When the meat is done to your liking, transfer it to a carving board. Cover the roast loosely with aluminum foil and let it rest for 10–20 minutes. Place individual plates on the stove top to warm from the heat of the oven. To carve a bone-in roast, use a carving knife or a chef's knife to cut between the ribs to make thick slices. For a boneless roast, slice the meat across the grain into slices ¼–½ inch (6–12 mm) thick. For more details on carving roasts, turn to page 43. Serve the sliced meat on the warmed plates with some pan juices spooned over the top.

1 bone-in or boneless veal loin roast, 4–5 lb (2–2.5 kg)

For the paste

4 cloves garlic, minced (page 33)

1 tablespoon minced fresh tarragon (page 34)

2 teaspoons salt

1 teaspoon lemon pepper

1 tablespoon olive oil, plus extra for thinning

MAKES 6–8 SERVINGS

CHEF'S TIP
Veal is popular in Italian cookery. If you're having trouble finding it in your regular meat market, try a butcher shop in an Italian neighborhood.

Chateaubriand with Béarnaise Sauce

Cut from the middle of the tenderloin, where the muscle begins to flatten, chateaubriand is an ideal centerpiece for a special-occasion dinner. Here, it is paired with an easy version of classic French béarnaise sauce, made from a tarragon-scented wine reduction, egg yolks, and butter.

2 pieces chateaubriand cut from the beef tenderloin, 2–3 inches (5–7.5 cm) thick and about 1 lb (500 g) each

2 tablespoons olive oil

2 teaspoons salt

1 teaspoon freshly ground pepper

For the quick béarnaise sauce

¼ cup (2 fl oz/60 ml) white wine vinegar

¼ cup (2 fl oz/60 ml) dry white wine such as Sauvignon Blanc

2 tablespoons minced fresh tarragon (page 34)

1 large shallot, minced (page 32)

4 large egg yolks

½ cup (4 oz/125 g) cold unsalted butter, cut into small pieces

1 teaspoon salt

½ teaspoon freshly ground pepper

MAKES 4 SERVINGS

CHEF'S TIP
Many butchers sell pieces of top sirloin cut 2 inches (5 cm) thick as chateaubriand. This cut is also very tender and can be cooked in the same way as the tenderloin.

1 **Trim and season the meat**
If you need help trimming a tenderloin, turn to page 39. Trim all the fat and silver skin from the meat. Rub the meat on all sides with 1 tablespoon of the olive oil, and sprinkle evenly with the salt and pepper. Put the meat on a plate and let stand at room temperature for 30–60 minutes before roasting.

2 **Make the béarnaise sauce**
In a small, nonreactive saucepan over high heat, combine the vinegar, wine, tarragon, and shallot. Cook until reduced to 2 tablespoons, about 5 minutes. Pour into a stainless-steel bowl fit snugly over (but not touching) gently bubbling water in a saucepan. Whisk the egg yolks into the wine mixture. Heat, whisking constantly, until the mixture begins to thicken, 2–3 minutes. Remove from the heat and whisk in the butter 1 or 2 pieces at a time, to form a thick sauce. Whisk in the salt and pepper. Remove from the heat, cover the bowl with aluminum foil, and keep warm over the hot water.

3 **Preheat the oven and brown the meat**
For more details about browning meat, turn to page 37. At least 15 minutes before you start cooking, position a rack in the middle of the oven and preheat to 400°F (200°C). Choose an ovenproof pan in which the meat fits with about 1 inch (2.5 cm) of space around each piece. Place the pan on the stove top over high heat. When the pan is hot, add the remaining 1 tablespoon olive oil and warm until the oil appears to shimmer. Put the meat pieces in the pan and cook, using tongs to turn them, until golden brown on all sides, 2–3 minutes on each side. Transfer the pan to the oven.

4 **Check the meat for doneness and let it rest**
For more details on checking meat for doneness, turn to page 42. Although the total roasting time is 20–30 minutes, it can vary depending on the thickness of the meat. Start checking early to prevent overdone meat. After 15 minutes, insert an instant-read thermometer into the center of each piece of meat; it should register 120°F (49°C) for rare or 130°F (54°C) for medium-rare. If the meat isn't ready, continue to roast for 5–10 minutes longer, and check again. When the meat is done, transfer it to a carving board, cover loosely with foil, and let rest for 5 minutes. Place plates on the stove top to warm from the heat of the oven.

5 **Carve the meat and serve**
Using a carving knife and fork, cut the meat across the grain ½ inch (12 mm) thick. Whisk the béarnaise sauce, spoon it over the meat, and serve right away.

Sautéed and Stir-fried Beef & Veal

On the pages that follow, you'll learn three closely related techniques for cooking thin, tender pieces of beef and veal: sautéing, pan-searing, and stir-frying. All three share the elements of quickly cooking medallions, steaks, or slices of meat in a small amount of fat over high heat. These techniques diverge, however, when it comes to timing and to the best pan to use.

Beef Medallions with Simple Pan Sauce

Here, beef medallions, tenderloin cut into thin rounds, are coated with a savory herb rub, then cooked quickly in a hot frying pan. All the flavor from cooking is utilized when you make a sauce from the browned bits on the bottom of the pan and the meat juices.

1 Trim the meat

If you are not sure how to trim a tenderloin, turn to page 39. Put the meat on a cutting board and find the thin end of the tenderloin; this is called the *tail*. Using a rigid boning knife or a chef's knife, trim off the tail and reserve it for another use. The tenderloin should now be 10–12 inches (25–30 cm) long. Using the same knife, trim all the fat from the exterior of the meat. Notice the thin, white membrane on the outside of the meat; this is called the *silver skin*. It should be trimmed, or it can cause the meat to curl as it cooks. To trim the silver skin, slide a thin, sharp knife, preferably a boning knife, under it at one end of the tenderloin. Keeping the knife pointed slightly upward and pulling the silver skin taut with your other hand, cut along the silver skin to separate it from the meat.

2 Cut the meat into medallions

Using a chef's knife, cut the tenderloin crosswise into 8 slices ¾–1 inch (2–2.5 cm) thick. These coin-shaped pieces of meat are known as *medallions*.

3 Coat the meat with the herb rub

In a small bowl, using a wooden spoon, mix together the paprika, garlic powder, thyme, tarragon, salt, and pepper, breaking up any paprika clumps with the back of the spoon. Using a pastry brush, brush the meat slices on all sides with 1 tablespoon of the olive oil. Sprinkle the herb mixture evenly over the oil-coated slices and press it in with your fingers (the oil will help it adhere). Put the slices on a plate, cover with plastic wrap, and let stand at room temperature for at least 30 minutes and up to 1 hour. Standing at room temperature allows the meat to absorb the flavors of the herb rub and it also encourages even cooking. ›

1 whole beef tenderloin, 6½–7 lb (3.25–3.5 kg)

2 tablespoons sweet paprika

1 tablespoon *each* garlic powder, dried thyme, and dried tarragon

2 teaspoons salt

1 teaspoon freshly ground pepper

2 tablespoons olive oil

For the simple pan sauce

4 shallots

2 cloves garlic

12 sprigs fresh flat-leaf (Italian) parsley

1 tablespoon unsalted butter

1 cup (8 fl oz/250 ml) Roasted Meat Stock (page 20)

2 tablespoons balsamic vinegar

1 tablespoon tomato paste

1 teaspoon Worcestershire sauce

1 teaspoon salt

½ teaspoon freshly ground pepper

¼ cup (2 fl oz/60 ml) heavy (double) cream, optional

MAKES 4 SERVINGS

4>

4 Prepare the ingredients for the sauce

To find out more about working with shallots, garlic, and parsley, turn to pages 32, 33, and 35. First, use a chef's knife to dice the shallot finely and measure out 2 tablespoons. Next, peel and mince the garlic, then measure out 1 tablespoon. Finally, pluck the parsley leaves from the stems, mince the leaves, and then measure out 1 tablespoon.

5 Choose a frying pan

Select a large, nonstick frying pan in which the steaks will fit in a single layer, with about 1 inch (2.5 cm) of space around each one. Selecting the proper-sized pan is critical for the searing process; a pan that is too large can cause the meat to burn, while a pan that is too small can cause it to steam. For details on easy measuring of pans using parchment (baking) paper, see page 12.

6 Cook the medallions

Preheat the oven to 200°F (95°C) and put a platter and 4 serving plates in the oven to warm. Place the pan on the stove top over medium-high heat. When it feels hot (you'll feel the heat rising upward when you hold your hand over it), add the remaining 1 tablespoon olive oil and heat until the surface appears to shimmer. Immediately add the medallions to the pan and cook, using tongs to turn them once or twice, for 5–6 minutes. As the medallions cook, they will turn dark golden brown on the surface. Remove from the heat.

7 Test the medallions for doneness

Because the medallions are relatively thin, testing them for doneness with a thermometer is not as practical as it is with thicker pieces. Using a paring knife, cut into a medallion and gauge its doneness visually: Rare meat will be deep red at the center; medium-rare meat will be deep pink at the center. For more details on judging doneness visually, turn to page 42. If the medallions are not done to your liking, put the pan back on the heat and cook them for a few minutes longer; they will probably take 6–8 minutes total to cook.

CHEF'S TIP

If you don't have a pan that is big enough to hold all the medallions at once, cook them in batches, and keep the first batch warm with the plates in the preheated oven.

8 Let the medallions rest

When the medallions are done to your liking, transfer them to the warmed platter, loosely cover with aluminum foil, and let them rest while you prepare the sauce. The meat will continue to cook slightly from the residual heat.

CHEF'S TIP

Enriching, or finishing, a sauce with cream adds a bit more fat, but it gives the sauce a luscious, velvety quality. Always use heavy (double) cream for this step. Its high fat content keeps it from curdling at high temperatures.

9 Cook the shallots, garlic, and parsley for the sauce

Put the frying pan back on the stove top over medium-high heat. Add the butter to the pan juices and stir with a wooden spoon until the butter is melted. Then stir in the shallots, garlic, and parsley and cook, stirring often, until the shallots are translucent and starting to brown, 3–4 minutes.

10 Deglaze the pan and reduce the sauce

With the heat still at medium-high, pour in the stock and vinegar and bring to a boil, scraping up the browned bits on the bottom and sides of the pan with a wooden spatula; this technique is called *deglazing.* (For more details on deglazing, turn to page 43.) These browned bits, or *fond,* will add good flavor to the final sauce. Once the liquid has absorbed the *fond,* let it cook until reduced by half, about 5 minutes; the timing will depend on the size of the pan. Tilt the pan occasionally to estimate the amount of liquid remaining. Reduce the heat to medium and stir in the tomato paste and Worcestershire sauce.

11 Adjust the seasonings

Stir in the salt and pepper, then taste the sauce. If it tastes a little flat, add a bit more salt, pepper, or vinegar to perk up the flavors. Remove the pan from the heat. If you prefer a richer sauce, briskly stir in the cream. Return the medallions to the pan and turn to evenly coat them in the sauce.

12 Serve the medallions

Put 2 medallions on each of the warmed plates. Use a spoon to pour the sauce over the steaks, dividing it evenly. Serve the sauced steaks right away.

Serving ideas

A sauce should seamlessly complement the dish it accompanies, neither overwhelming the meat nor being overshadowed by it. Keep this in mind when you serve sauces with your beef or veal. You don't want to drown your meat in the sauce, or the true flavor of the meat won't shine through. Here are three ways to serve a sauce attractively. These same ideas can be applied to many other types of dishes that are served with a sauce.

Medallions on a pool of sauce (top left)
To show off perfectly browned medallions, spoon a little sauce onto a warmed plate. Use the back of the spoon to spread the sauce in a thin, even layer. Put the medallions on top of the sauce, and garnish with a fresh herb used in the sauce.

Medallions with sauce on the side (left)
Presenting the sauce in a sauceboat allows your guests to choose how much sauce they want.

Medallions drizzled with sauce (above)
Arrange the medallions on a warmed platter, drizzle the sauce over the top of the meat, and garnish with a sprig of a fresh herb used in the sauce. Pass the platter at the table.

Beef Medallions Variations

After learning how to prepare the Beef Medallions with Simple Pan Sauce on page 67, and feeling at ease with the techniques of cooking medallions, deglazing a pan, and reducing a sauce, you can try these variations. They use the same techniques, but call for different ingredients to create new sauces or herb rubs. The only difference between the beef medallions and the veal scaloppine, or thin veal scallops, in two of these variations is that the latter are lightly coated with flour before they are browned. Veal scaloppine dishes are generally served with a sauce based on wine or tomatoes, as they are here in the Veal Marsala and Veal Piccata. Each variation makes 4 servings.

Beef Medallions with Madeira Sauce

If you like a more complex and elegant dish, use a fortified wine such as Madeira in the pan sauce.

Trim 1 beef tenderloin (6½–7 lb/ 3.25–3.5 kg) and cut into medallions.

Next, in a small bowl, mix together 2 tablespoons sweet paprika and 1 tablespoon *each* garlic powder, dried thyme, and dried marjoram. Brush the beef with 1 tablespoon olive oil and rub the herb mixture all over the meat. Let stand for 30–60 minutes.

In a large, nonstick frying pan over medium-high heat, warm 1 tablespoon olive oil. When hot, add the medallions and cook until done to your liking, 5–8 minutes. Transfer the medallions to a plate and deglaze the pan with ¼ cup (2 fl oz/60 ml) Madeira such as Malmsey. Reduce by half, then stir in 1 tablespoon tomato paste and 1 teaspoon Worcestershire sauce. If desired, whisk in ¼ cup (2 fl oz/60 ml) heavy (double) cream. Adjust the seasonings, then serve with the medallions.

Beef Medallions with Mushroom Sauce

The earthy flavor of the mushrooms complements the beef in this dish.

Trim 1 beef tenderloin (6½–7 lb/ 3.25–3.5 kg) and cut into medallions.

Next, in a small bowl, mix together 2 tablespoons sweet paprika and 1 tablespoon *each* garlic powder, dried thyme, and dried rosemary. Brush the beef with 1 tablespoon olive oil and rub the herb mixture all over the meat. Let stand for 30–60 minutes.

In a large, nonstick frying pan over medium-high heat, warm 1 tablespoon olive oil. When hot, add the medallions and cook until done to your liking, 5–8 minutes. Transfer to a plate. Melt 2 tablespoons unsalted butter in the pan. Stir in 2 tablespoons minced shallot and ½ lb (250 g) sliced fresh mushrooms (shiitake, morel, chanterelle, or a mixture) and sauté until lightly browned, 4–6 minutes. Deglaze with 1 cup (8 fl oz/ 250 ml) Roasted Meat Stock (page 20) and ¼ cup (2 fl oz/60 ml) dry sherry. Reduce by half, then stir in 1 tablespoon tomato paste and 1 teaspoon Worcestershire sauce. Adjust the seasonings, then serve with the medallions.

Veal Medallions with Mustard Cream Sauce

Here, medallions are cut from veal loin instead of beef and paired with a tangy mustard sauce made from the pan juices.

Trim 1 veal top loin (6½–7 lb/3.25–3.5 kg) and cut into medallions.

Next, in a small bowl, mix together 1 tablespoon dry mustard, 1 tablespoon garlic powder, 1 tablespoon dried tarragon, 2 teaspoons salt, and 1 teaspoon freshly ground pepper. Brush the veal with 1 tablespoon olive oil and rub the herb mixture all over the meat. Let stand for 30–60 minutes.

In a large, nonstick frying pan over medium-high heat, heat 1 tablespoon olive oil. When hot, add the medallions and cook until done to your liking, 5–8 minutes. Transfer to a plate. Melt 1 tablespoon unsalted butter in the pan. Stir in 2 tablespoons minced shallot and 1 tablespoon chopped fresh flat-leaf (Italian) parsley and sauté until the shallot starts to brown, 3–4 minutes. Deglaze with 1 cup (8 fl oz/ 250 ml) Chicken Stock (page 22) and 1 tablespoon Dijon mustard. Reduce by half, then whisk in ¼ cup (2 fl oz/60 ml) heavy (double) cream. Adjust the seasonings, then serve with the medallions.

Beef Medallions en Croûte with Truffle Sauce

The flavor of the truffles in the oil is so distinctive, you won't need an herb rub for this recipe.

Trim 1 beef tenderloin (6½–7 lb/ 3.25–3.5 kg) and cut into medallions. Rub the meat with 1 tablespoon black or white truffle oil and season with 2 teaspoons salt and 1 teaspoon freshly ground pepper.

In a large, nonstick frying pan over medium-high heat, warm 1 tablespoon olive oil. When hot, add the medallions and cook until done to your liking, 5–8 minutes. Transfer the medallions to a plate. Melt 1 tablespoon unsalted butter in the pan. Stir in 2 tablespoons coarsely chopped black truffles and sauté until the truffles soften, 3–4 minutes. Deglaze the pan with 1 cup (8 fl oz/250 ml) Roasted Meat Stock (page 20) and ¼ cup (2 fl oz/ 60 ml) tawny port. Reduce by half, then stir in 1 teaspoon salt and ½ teaspoon freshly ground pepper. Remove the pan from the heat and whisk in 2 tablespoons unsalted butter. Adjust the seasonings.

Meanwhile, in a large frying pan over medium-high heat, warm 2 tablespoons olive oil and add 8 small portobello mushroom caps. Cook, turning once, until they are browned and starting to soften, 2–3 minutes per side. Transfer to a plate and cover with aluminum foil to keep warm.

To serve, drizzle 8 slices toasted French bread (½ inch/12 mm thick) with 1 tablespoon black or white truffle oil. Top each with a beef medallion, then a mushroom cap, and spoon the sauce over the top.

Veal Piccata

Scaloppine, which are thinner versions of medallions, are about ¼ inch (6 mm) thick. They are available, already cut, at quality butcher shops.

In a shallow dish, mix together 1 cup (5 oz/155 g) all-purpose (plain) flour, 1 tablespoon dried oregano, 1 tablespoon garlic powder, 2 teaspoons salt, and 1 teaspoon freshly ground pepper. Dredge 1 lb (500 g) veal scaloppine in the seasoned flour, being sure to coat all sides. Shake each piece to remove the excess flour and put on a plate.

In a large frying pan over medium-high heat, warm 2 tablespoons olive oil. When hot, add the veal and cook, turning once, until golden brown, 30–60 seconds per side. Transfer to a warmed platter and cover loosely with aluminum foil.

Deglaze the pan with ½ cup (4 fl oz/125 ml) dry white wine such as Pinot Grigio and ½ cup (4 fl oz/125 ml) Chicken Stock (page 22). Reduce by half, then stir in 2 tablespoons rinsed and drained capers (preferably nonpareil), and the juice of 1 lemon. Stir in 1 teaspoon salt and ½ teaspoon freshly ground pepper. Adjust the seasonings.

Serve the veal with the sauce spooned over the top. Sprinkle each serving with 1 tablespoon minced fresh flat-leaf (Italian) parsley and top with 12 thin lemon slices, dividing evenly.

Veal Marsala

This classic Italian sauce, thick with meaty mushrooms, is a good partner for mild veal scaloppine.

In a shallow dish, mix together 1 cup (5 oz/155 g) all-purpose (plain) flour, 1 tablespoon dried oregano, 1 tablespoon garlic powder, 2 teaspoons salt, and 1 teaspoon freshly ground pepper. Dredge 1 lb (500 g) veal scaloppine in the seasoned flour, being sure to coat all sides. Shake each piece to remove the excess flour and put on a plate.

In a large frying pan over medium-high heat, warm 2 tablespoons olive oil. When hot, add the veal and cook, turning once, until golden brown, 30–60 seconds per side. Transfer to a warmed platter and cover loosely with aluminum foil.

Add 1 tablespoon olive oil to the pan over medium-high heat. When hot, add 1 cup (3 oz/90 g) chopped fresh white or brown mushrooms and sauté until lightly browned, 3–4 minutes. Deglaze the pan with 1 cup (8 fl oz/250 ml) Marsala wine and 1 cup (8 fl oz/250 ml) Chicken Stock (page 22). Reduce by half, then stir in 1 tablespoon tomato paste. If the sauce seems too thick, thin it with a little more Marsala. Add 1 teaspoon salt and ½ teaspoon freshly ground pepper. Adjust the seasonings.

Serve the veal with the sauce spooned over the top. Sprinkle each serving with 1 tablespoon minced fresh flat-leaf (Italian) parsley.

Stir-fried Sesame Beef

Top-sirloin steak, cut from the little-exercised sirloin portion of the steer, is a perfect cut for stir-frying. The already tender meat cooks quickly in the hot wok and stays succulent because of a marinade. Fresh snow peas and green onions add color and crunch.

1 Trim and slice the beef
To prepare the meat for stir-frying, using a rigid boning knife or a chef's knife, trim away any fat on the edges of the meat and remove any nuggets of fat or pieces of connective tissue. You remove all the fat because it isn't needed to moisturize the meat; the marinade will provide plenty of moisture along with flavor. Use the chef's knife to cut the beef across the grain into slices ¼ inch (6 mm) thick and 2 inches (5 cm) long. Put the beef in a shallow glass or ceramic dish.

2 Prepare the snow peas and green onions
Most snow peas today are string free, but if there are any strings, pull them off and discard them. Cut off the white parts of the green onions and reserve them for another use. Using the green parts only, cut the onions at an angle to match the length of the snow peas. Put the snow peas and green onions in a bowl and place them near the stove so you can easily reach them.

3 Mince the garlic and ginger for the marinade
If you are new to mincing garlic and ginger, turn to pages 33 and 36. Place the garlic clove on a work surface, firmly press against it with the flat side of a chef's knife, and pull away the papery skin. Rock the knife over the garlic to mince it. Using a vegetable peeler, remove the thin beige skin from the ginger, and then use the chef's knife to cut it into coin-shaped slices, then strips. Cut the strips into small pieces, then mince. Measure out 1 tablespoon.

4 Marinate the beef
In a small bowl, stir together the garlic, ginger, soy sauce, rice vinegar, sesame oil, sesame seeds, and five-spice powder. Pour the marinade over the beef in the dish and turn the beef to coat evenly. Cover and let stand at room temperature for 30 minutes, turning the meat occasionally. Marinating infuses the meat with flavors and helps tenderize and moisturize it. >

1½ lb (750 g) top-sirloin steak

1 cup (3 oz/90 g) snow peas (mangetouts)

8 green (spring) onions

For the marinade

1 clove garlic

1-inch (2.5-cm) piece fresh ginger

2 tablespoons reduced-sodium soy sauce

1 tablespoon rice vinegar

1 tablespoon Asian sesame oil

1½ tablespoons sesame seeds

1 teaspoon five-spice powder

For the sauce

¼ cup (2 fl oz/60 ml) Roasted Meat Stock (page 20)

2 tablespoons reduced-sodium soy sauce

1 tablespoon cornstarch (cornflour)

1 tablespoon Chinese rice wine or dry sherry

2 teaspoons Asian sesame oil

2 tablespoons peanut or corn oil, plus extra if the beef is sticking

MAKES 4 SERVINGS

5 Make the sauce

In a small bowl, using a fork, stir together the stock, soy sauce, and cornstarch until the cornstarch is completely dissolved. Use the tines of the fork to press and crush any clumps of cornstarch against the side of the bowl. Using a whisking motion, mix in the rice wine and sesame oil. Set the sauce near the stove so you can easily reach it.

6 Ready your equipment and ingredients

Before you begin stir-frying, make sure you have everything you need (your *mise en place*; see page 12) prepared and ready at hand, as you will need to cook the dish quickly. Preheat the oven to 200°F (95°C) and place individual plates in the oven to warm. Have ready a wok, preferably about 14 inches (35 cm) in diameter, and 2 wooden spatulas or long-handled spoons. Stir-frying can generate smoke, so be sure to turn on your oven ventilation or use a fan to circulate the air.

CHEF'S TIP

Stir-frying, the rapid tossing and stirring of small pieces of food in hot oil over high heat, preserves the fresh flavor, texture, and color of ingredients. Chinese chefs advise "hot wok, cold oil." In other words, get your wok as hot as possible before adding the cold oil, and then get the oil searing hot before adding the other ingredients.

7 Heat the wok

Place the wok over high heat. Hold your hand over the pan. When you feel the heat rising upward, add 1 tablespoon of the peanut oil and carefully tilt and rotate the pan so that the oil is distributed over the pan's surface and is hot.

8 Stir-fry the beef

Immediately add the meat with the marinade to the wok, spreading it out over the surface. Let it cook undisturbed for 20–30 seconds to brown on one side, then stir vigorously with the spatulas or spoons, moving the meat over the surface of the pan and up the sides, to expose it evenly to the heat. Add a little more peanut oil if it seems like the meat is sticking. Cook, constantly stirring and tossing the meat in the wok, until the meat is browned on all sides; this will take 1–3 minutes. Keep the meat constantly moving in the pan so that it doesn't burn. (If you are using a wok or pan less than 14 inches in diameter, cook the meat in 2 batches to avoid crowding the pan, which will cause the meat to steam.) Transfer the meat to a plate and cover it with aluminum foil to keep warm. >

9 Stir-fry the vegetables

Put the wok back over high heat. When it is hot (hold your hand over it to test the heat), add the remaining 1 tablespoon peanut oil and tilt to coat the surface of the pan and heat briefly. Add the snow peas and the green onions and cook, stirring and tossing constantly, until the snow peas and green onions are bright green and lightly crunchy, 3–4 minutes. If you like your vegetables less crunchy, add 1 tablespoon water, cover, and cook for 1–2 minutes longer.

10 Add the sauce

Quickly whisk the sauce again to recombine all the ingredients. Return the reserved beef and any accumulated juices to the wok and quickly toss with the vegetables. Pour the sauce into the wok and, using the spatulas or spoons, stir the mixture into the beef. Stir vigorously until the sauce thickens and coats the meat, snow peas, and green onions and the mixture looks brown and glossy, about 30 seconds. Stir-fried beef cooks so quickly that it's difficult to test it for doneness in the same way as you do with other cooking techniques. When done properly, stir-fried beef is medium-rare to medium; sample a piece to make sure it is done to your liking.

11 Adjust the seasonings

As you taste the piece of beef, also note the flavors; they should be a bold, balanced mixture of salty, sweet, sour, and spicy, with nutty notes from the sesame seeds and oil. They should not be so strong that they overpower the beef, however. You can stir in a little more soy sauce if needed to perk up the flavors.

12 Serve the stir-fry

Divide the stir-fry among the warmed plates and serve right away.

Finishing touches

A few simple ingredients added to any stir-fry right before serving can heighten the colors, textures, and flavors of the finished dish. For example, green onions and sesame seeds are both used earlier in this dish, so adding an additional small amount at the end is a perfect way to layer the flavors. A sprinkle of finely chopped red bell pepper adds a contrasting color and a pleasing and fresh crunch to the dish.

Slivered green onions (top left)
Cut trimmed green (spring) onions lengthwise into thin strips. Put the strips in a bowl of ice water until they start to curl. Shake off the excess water from the curled onions and use to garnish the stir-fry.

Diced red bell peppers (left)
Using a chef's knife, cut a seeded red bell pepper (capsicum) into strips ⅛ inch (6 mm) wide. Line up the strips and cut crosswise into ⅛-inch dice. Sprinkle a small amount over each serving.

Sesame seeds (above)
Toast 1 tablespoon sesame seeds in a dry frying pan over medium-low heat until lightly browned and fragrant. Sprinkle a small amount over each serving.

Stir-fried Beef Variations

The trio of basic techniques—cutting and marinating the beef; heating the wok and then the oil; and the rapid stirring, tossing, and cooking of all the ingredients in the hot pan—you have mastered in Stir-fried Sesame Beef (page 75) can now be applied to other combinations of beef and vegetables or, in some cases, even fruit. It is easy to give these quick dishes an Asian flavor by using some of the many fresh and prepared products now available on the shelves and in the produce sections of supermarkets, including bok choy, Chinese oyster sauce and black bean sauce, Southeast Asian lemongrass, and Thai curry paste. Each variation makes 4 servings.

Beef & Broccoli with Oyster Sauce

This recipe calls for a garlicky marinade and features crisp broccoli in place of the snow peas.

Trim 1½ lb (750 g) top-sirloin steak and cut into slices ¼ inch (6 mm) thick and 2 inches (5 cm) long. Next, cut 10 oz (315 g) broccoli into bite-sized florets.

In a small bowl, combine 1 chopped garlic clove, 1 tablespoon chopped fresh ginger, 2 tablespoons reduced-sodium soy sauce, and 1 teaspoon Asian sesame oil and mix well. Put the beef in a shallow glass dish, pour the mixture over it, and marinate for 30 minutes.

Make a sauce by whisking together ¼ cup (2 fl oz/60 ml) Roasted Meat Stock (page 20), 3 tablespoons oyster sauce, 2 tablespoons reduced-sodium soy sauce, 1 tablespoon Chinese rice wine or dry sherry, 1 tablespoon cornstarch (cornflour), and 2 teaspoons Asian sesame oil.

Place all your ingredients near the stove, including 2 tablespoons peanut or corn oil. Starting at step 7, stir-fry the beef and vegetables, then add the sauce. Adjust the seasonings and serve right away.

Beef & Green Beans in Black Bean Sauce

Here, a store-bought Chinese sauce made from fermented soybeans and garlic lends its bold flavor to a beef stir-fry.

Trim 1½ lb (750 g) top-sirloin steak and cut into slices ¼ inch (6 mm) thick and 2 inches (5 cm) long. Next, cut 1 lb (500 g) green beans on the diagonal into bite-sized pieces.

In a small bowl, combine 2 tablespoons reduced-sodium soy sauce, 1 tablespoon Chinese black bean sauce, and 4 finely chopped garlic cloves and mix well. Put the beef in a shallow glass dish, pour the mixture over it, and marinate for 30 minutes.

Make a sauce by whisking together ¼ cup (2 fl oz/60 ml) water and 1 tablespoon cornstarch (cornflour) until smooth; then stir in ¼ cup (2 fl oz/60 ml) Chinese black bean sauce.

Place all your ingredients near the stove, including 2 tablespoons peanut or corn oil. Starting at step 7, stir-fry the beef and vegetables, then add the sauce. Adjust the seasonings and serve right away.

Lemongrass Beef with Bok Choy

This Southeast Asian–inspired dish pairs citrusy lemongrass and bold fish sauce.

Trim 1½ lb (750 g) top-sirloin steak and cut into slices ¼ inch (6 mm) thick and 2 inches (5 cm) long. Next, coarsely chop 1 lb (500 g) bok choy.

In a small bowl, combine 2 tablespoons reduced-sodium soy sauce, 1 tablespoon Asian fish sauce, 1 tablespoon peanut oil, 1 tablespoon Chinese rice wine or dry sherry, 4 finely chopped garlic cloves, 1 teaspoon red pepper flakes, and 2 finely chopped lemongrass stalks (bulblike base only) and mix well. Put the beef in a shallow glass dish, pour the mixture over it, and marinate for 30 minutes.

Make a sauce by whisking together ¼ cup (2 fl oz/60 ml) Roasted Meat Stock (page 20), 2 tablespoons reduced sodium soy sauce, 2 tablespoons fish sauce, 1 tablespoon fresh lime juice, 1 tablespoon cornstarch (cornflour), and 1 teaspoon Asian sesame oil.

Place all your ingredients near the stove, including 2 tablespoons peanut or corn oil. Starting at step 7, stir-fry the beef and vegetables, then add the sauce. Adjust the seasonings and serve right away.

Tangerine Beef

The bright color and flavor of tangerines are paired with the beef in this stir-fry.

Trim 1½ lb (750 g) top-sirloin steak and cut into slices ¼ inch (6 mm) thick and 2 inches (5 cm) long. Next, peel, section, and seed 3 tangerines or oranges.

In a small bowl, combine 2 tablespoons finely chopped tangerine or orange zest, 2 tablespoons reduced-sodium soy sauce, ¼ cup (2 fl oz/60 ml) fresh tangerine or orange juice, 1½ teaspoons minced fresh ginger, 1 teaspoon Asian sesame oil, and 1 teaspoon red pepper flakes and mix well. Put the beef in a shallow glass dish, pour the mixture over it, and marinate for 30 minutes.

Make a sauce by whisking together ¼ cup (2 fl oz/60 ml) Roasted Meat Stock (page 20), 2 tablespoons Chinese rice wine or dry sherry, 1 tablespoon reduced-sodium soy sauce, 2 teaspoons cornstarch (cornflour), 2 finely chopped green (spring) onions (white and pale green parts), and ½ seeded and finely chopped serrano chile. Stir in the tangerine sections.

Place all your ingredients near the stove, including 1 tablespoon peanut or corn oil. Stir-fry the beef in the oil, then add the sauce and stir-fry until the sauce is thickened and the beef is coated. Adjust the seasonings and serve right away.

Vietnamese Beef & Watercress

This recipe is based on a traditional Vietnamese dish called shaking beef.

Trim 1½ lb (750 g) top-sirloin steak and cut into slices ¼ inch (6 mm) thick and 2 inches (5 cm) long. Next, remove the large stems from 1¼ lb (625 g) watercress and cut it into 2-inch (5-cm) pieces.

In a small bowl, combine 2 tablespoons reduced-sodium soy sauce, 1 tablespoon corn oil, 2 teaspoons fresh lime juice, 2 teaspoons fish sauce, 6 chopped garlic cloves, and 1 teaspoon red pepper flakes and mix well. Put the beef in a shallow glass dish, pour the mixture over it, and marinate for 30 minutes.

Make a sauce by whisking together 2 tablespoons reduced-sodium soy sauce, 2 tablespoons rice vinegar, 1 tablespoon Chinese rice wine or dry sherry, 2 teaspoons fresh lime juice, 1½ teaspoons Asian fish sauce, 1 teaspoon Asian sesame oil, 2 chopped green (spring) onions (white and tender green parts), and ½ teaspoon freshly ground pepper. Add 1 thinly sliced red onion and let the onion marinate for 30 minutes. Strain the sauce, reserving the red onion.

Place all your ingredients near the stove, including 1 tablespoon peanut or corn oil. Stir-fry the beef in the oil, then add the marinated onion and stir-fry until tender-crisp, about 1 minute.

In a large bowl, toss the watercress with the reserved sauce and divide among 4 warmed plates. Top with the stir-fried onion and beef. Adjust the seasonings, garnish with 4 lime quarters, and serve right away.

Thai Red Curry Beef

Here, prepared Thai red curry paste flavors beef and mixed vegetables.

Trim 1½ lb (750 g) top-sirloin steak and cut into slices ¼ inch (6 mm) thick and 2 inches (5 cm) long. Next, coarsely chop 1 yellow onion, 1 red bell pepper (capsicum), and 3 plum (Roma) tomatoes. Peel 2 carrots and cut into thin slices. Finally, mince 2 cloves garlic and 1 tablespoon fresh ginger.

Make a sauce by whisking together 1–2 tablespoons Thai red curry paste and ¼ cup (2 fl oz/60 ml) Roasted Meat Stock (page 20).

Place all your ingredients near the stove, including 2 tablespoons peanut or corn oil. Stir-fry the beef in 1 tablespoon oil, then transfer to a plate. Put the wok back over high heat and add another 1 tablespoon oil. When hot, add the onion and carrots and stir-fry until softened, about 2 minutes. Add the garlic, ginger, bell pepper, tomatoes, and sauce and stir-fry until well mixed and bubbling, about 2 minutes.

Return the beef to the wok along with 1 can (13½ fl oz/415 ml) unsweetened coconut milk and 10 fresh basil leaves. Bring to a boil, stirring constantly, then remove from the heat. Adjust the seasonings and serve right away.

Pan-Seared Steak with Marchand de Vin Sauce

Here, boneless strip steaks, which come from the sirloin portion of the steer, or rib-eye steaks, from the rib section, are quickly seared over high heat to create a savory crust and a juicy interior. Pan-searing allows you to use the cooking juices for a flavorful sauce, like this classic French recipe featuring red wine and parsley.

4 boneless strip steaks or rib-eye steaks, 1 inch (2.5 cm) thick

2 tablespoons olive oil

2 teaspoons salt

1 teaspoon freshly ground pepper

For the sauce

1 tablespoon unsalted butter, plus 2 tablespoons for finishing the sauce, optional

2 tablespoons minced shallot (page 32)

2 tablespoons minced fresh flat-leaf (Italian) parsley (page 35)

1 cup (8 fl oz/250 ml) Roasted Meat Stock (page 20)

½ cup (4 fl oz/125 ml) dry red wine such as Zinfandel

1 teaspoon salt

½ teaspoon freshly ground pepper

MAKES 4 SERVINGS

CHEF'S TIP

If your steaks are more than 1 inch (2.5 cm) thick, you can use a modified cooking method, pan-roasting. Use an ovenproof frying pan to brown the steaks on one side, about 2 minutes. Turn over the steaks and put them, still in the pan, into a preheated 400°F (200°C) oven for about 5 minutes, and then test for doneness and continue with the recipe.

1 **Trim and season the steaks**
If you are not sure how to trim steaks, turn to page 38. Trim the steaks, leaving ¼ inch (6 mm) of fat on the edges. Cut 2 or 3 shallow slashes in the fat on each steak. (If using rib-eye steaks, cut out the nugget of fat found in the center of the steak.) Put the steaks on a plate, brush both sides with 1 tablespoon of the olive oil, and sprinkle with the salt and pepper. Let the meat stand at room temperature for 30–60 minutes before cooking.

2 **Brown the steaks**
Preheat the oven to 200°F (95°C) and put a platter and individual plates in the oven to warm. Select a large, nonstick frying pan in which the steaks will fit in a single layer, with about 1 inch (2.5 cm) of space around each one. Place the pan on the stove top over medium-high heat. When hot, add the remaining 1 tablespoon olive oil and heat until the surface appears to shimmer. Add the steaks and cook, turning once, until they are golden brown and crusty on both sides, about 2 minutes on each side.

3 **Test the steaks for doneness**
If you need help checking meat for doneness, turn to page 42. Insert an instant-read thermometer into the center of the meat; it should register 120°F (49°C) for rare or 130°F (54°C) for medium-rare. If they are not yet done to your liking, cook for 1–2 minutes longer on each side and test again. Transfer the steaks to the platter, cover loosely with aluminum foil, and let rest for 3–5 minutes.

4 **Make the sauce**
Return the pan to medium heat. Add the 1 tablespoon butter to the pan juices. When the butter has melted, stir in the shallot and parsley and cook, stirring often, until the shallot is translucent, 3–4 minutes. Stir in the stock and wine, raise the heat to medium-high, and scrape up the browned bits on the bottom of the pan to *deglaze* it. (For more details on deglazing, turn to page 43.) Continue to cook until reduced by half, 5–7 minutes. Remove from the heat, stir in the salt and pepper, and taste the sauce. If it tastes a little flat, add a little more salt or pepper. If you prefer a richer sauce, whisk in the 2 tablespoons butter.

5 **Serve the steaks**
Divide the steaks among the warmed plates and spoon the sauce over them, dividing it evenly. Serve the steaks right away.

Pan-Seared Steak Variations

Pan-searing thick, juicy steaks until their exterior is caramelized is one of the best ways to bring out the distinctive flavor of beef. You can make the most of the precious juices that are released during pan-searing by deglazing the pan with wine and/or stock. Once the liquid has reduced, you can enrich the pan sauce with cream or butter to make it even more luscious. You will recognize many favorite steak dishes in these variations, from the classic Steak Diane, with its creamy Cognac sauce, to piquant Steak au Poivre, with crunchy cracked black peppercorns. Each variation makes 4 servings.

Pan-Seared Steak with Horseradish Jus

Horseradish is a classic accompaniment to roast beef. Here, the pungent ingredient is made into a pan sauce to top the steaks.

Trim 4 boneless strip steaks or rib-eye steaks. Brush with 1 tablespoon olive oil, then season with 2 teaspoons salt and 1 teaspoon freshly ground pepper, dividing evenly. Let the steaks stand for 30–60 minutes.

In a large frying pan over medium-high heat, warm 1 tablespoon olive oil. When hot, add the steaks and cook until they are golden brown and crusty, about 2 minutes per side. Transfer the steaks to a plate to rest and deglaze the pan with 1 cup (8 fl oz/250 ml) Roasted Meat Stock (page 20). Reduce by half, then whisk in 2 tablespoons prepared horseradish, 1 tablespoon Worcestershire sauce, 1 teaspoon salt, and ½ teaspoon freshly ground pepper. Adjust the seasonings.

Serve the sauce spooned over the steaks.

Pan-Seared Steak with Classic Steakhouse Sauce

Reminiscent of the sauce served in old-style steakhouses, this easy pan sauce mingles many ingredients you probably already have in your pantry.

Trim 4 boneless strip steaks or rib-eye steaks. Brush with 1 tablespoon olive oil, then season with 2 teaspoons salt and 1 teaspoon freshly ground pepper, dividing evenly. Let the steaks stand for 30–60 minutes.

In a large frying pan over medium-high heat, warm 1 tablespoon olive oil. When hot, add the steaks and cook until golden brown and crusty, about 2 minutes per side. Transfer the steaks to a plate to rest and deglaze the pan with 1 cup (8 fl oz/ 250 ml) Roasted Meat Stock (page 20). Reduce by half, then whisk in 1 tablespoon prepared horseradish, 1 tablespoon tomato paste, ¼ cup (2 fl oz/ 60 ml) tomato ketchup, 2 tablespoons Dijon mustard, 1 tablespoon Worcestershire sauce, 1 teaspoon salt, and ½ teaspoon freshly ground pepper. Reduce the heat to medium and cook, whisking often, until thickened, about 5 minutes. Adjust the seasonings.

Serve the sauce spooned over the steaks.

Green Peppercorn Steak

In another classic pairing for pan-seared steaks, green peppercorns are combined with dry white wine.

Trim 4 boneless strip steaks or rib-eye steaks. Brush with 1 tablespoon olive oil, then season with 2 teaspoons salt, dividing evenly. Let the steaks stand for 30–60 minutes.

In a large frying pan over medium-high heat, warm 1 tablespoon olive oil. When hot, add the steaks and cook until golden brown and crusty, about 2 minutes per side. Transfer the steaks to a plate to rest. Add 1 tablespoon unsalted butter to the pan. When melted, add 2 tablespoons drained, rinsed, and crushed brine-packed green peppercorns, 2 tablespoons minced shallot, and 1 tablespoon chopped fresh flat-leaf (Italian) parsley and sauté until the shallot is translucent, 3–4 minutes. Deglaze with 1 cup (8 fl oz/250 ml) Roasted Meat Stock (page 20) and ½ cup (4 fl oz/125 ml) dry white wine such as Sauvignon Blanc. Reduce by half, then whisk in 1 teaspoon salt and ½ teaspoon freshly ground pepper. For extra richness, if desired, whisk in 2 tablespoons unsalted butter. Adjust the seasonings.

Serve the sauce spooned over the steaks.

Steak Diane

In this recipe, I've deepened the flavor of the traditional dish by coating the steaks with a mustard rub, which is echoed by the Dijon mustard in the sauce.

Trim 4 boneless strip steaks or rib-eye steaks. Next, in a bowl, mix together 2 teaspoons salt, 1 teaspoon freshly ground pepper, 2 tablespoons sweet paprika, 1 tablespoon dry mustard, and 1 tablespoon garlic powder. Brush the steaks with 1 tablespoon olive oil, then rub with the spice mixture. Let stand for 30–60 minutes.

In a large frying pan over medium-high heat, warm 1 tablespoon olive oil. When hot, add the steaks and cook until golden brown and crusty, about 2 minutes per side. Transfer the steaks to a plate to rest. Add 1 tablespoon unsalted butter to the pan. When melted, add 2 tablespoons minced shallot and 1 tablespoon minced fresh flat-leaf (Italian) parsley and sauté until the shallot is translucent, 3–4 minutes. Deglaze with 1 cup (8 fl oz/ 250 ml) Roasted Meat Stock (page 20) and reduce by half. Remove the pan from the heat and whisk in 2 tablespoons Cognac or other brandy, 2 tablespoons Dijon mustard, 1 tablespoon Worcestershire sauce, 1 teaspoon salt, and ½ teaspoon freshly ground pepper. Adjust the seasonings, then whisk in ¼ cup (2 fl oz/ 60 ml) heavy (double) cream.

Serve the sauce spooned over the steaks.

Steak au Poivre

Coating the steaks with cracked peppercorns contributes both texture and flavor, while the Cognac and cream add an elegant finish.

Trim 4 boneless strip steaks or rib-eye steaks. Next, place about 1 tablespoon peppercorns on a cutting board. Position a heavy pan on top of the peppercorns and apply pressure to the pan to crack them. Measure out 2 teaspoons cracked pepper. Brush the steaks with 1 tablespoon olive oil. Sprinkle with 1 teaspoon salt and press the cracked pepper into both sides of the meat, dividing evenly. Let stand for 30–60 minutes.

In a large frying pan over medium-high heat, warm 1 tablespoon olive oil. When hot, add the steaks and cook until golden brown and crusty, about 2 minutes per side. Transfer the steaks to a plate to rest. Add 2 tablespoons unsalted butter to the pan. When melted, add 2 tablespoons minced shallot and 1 tablespoon chopped fresh flat-leaf (Italian) parsley and sauté until the shallot is translucent, 3–4 minutes. Deglaze with 1 cup (8 fl oz/ 250 ml) Roasted Meat Stock (page 20) and reduce by half. Remove the pan from the heat and whisk in 2 tablespoons Cognac or other brandy, 1 tablespoon tomato paste, and 1 teaspoon salt. Adjust the seasonings, then whisk in ¼ cup (2 fl oz/60 ml) heavy (double) cream.

Serve the sauce spooned over the steaks.

Pan-Seared Steak with Warm Arugula Salad

Here, the pan juices are used to make a vinaigrette for tossing with greens that are served alongside the steaks.

Trim 4 boneless strip steaks or rib-eye steaks. Brush with 1 tablespoon olive oil and season with 1 teaspoon salt and 1 teaspoon lemon pepper, dividing evenly. Let stand for 30–60 minutes.

In a large frying pan over medium-high heat, warm 1 tablespoon olive oil. When hot, add the steaks and cook until golden brown and crusty, about 2 minutes per side. Transfer the steaks to a plate to rest. Add ¼ cup (2 fl oz/60 ml) olive oil to the pan. When hot, add 4 thinly sliced garlic cloves and sauté until translucent, 2–3 minutes. Deglaze with 2 tablespoons balsamic vinegar, ½ cup (4 fl oz/125 ml) dry red wine such as Zinfandel, and the juice of 1 lemon. Stir 1 teaspoon salt and ½ teaspoon freshly ground pepper into the warm vinaigrette. Adjust the seasonings.

To serve, toss 4 cups (4 oz/125 g) arugula (rocket) leaves with ¼ cup (2 fl oz/60 ml) of the warm vinaigrette until they wilt slightly. Divide the dressed greens among individual plates, top each with 1 steak, and pass the extra vinaigrette at the table.

2 lb (1 kg) beef tenderloin

For the rub

1 teaspoon dried tarragon

1 teaspoon dry mustard

1 teaspoon onion powder

2 teaspoons salt

1 teaspoon freshly ground pepper

1 tablespoon olive oil

1 lb (500 g) dried egg noodles

For the sauce

1 tablespoon olive oil

1 tablespoon unsalted butter

½ lb (250 g) fresh white or brown
mushrooms, brushed clean and thinly sliced

¼ cup (1 oz/30 g) diced yellow onion
(page 32)

1 tablespoon chopped fresh tarragon
(page 34)

1 cup (8 fl oz/250 ml) Roasted Meat Stock
(page 20)

2 tablespoons sweet mustard

½ cup (4 oz/125 g) sour cream

Dash of Worcestershire sauce

1 teaspoon salt

⅛ teaspoon freshly ground pepper

⅓ cup (⅓ oz/10 g) chopped fresh flat-leaf
(Italian) parsley (page 35)

MAKES 4 SERVINGS

Beef Stroganoff

I heighten the flavor of this classic dish by seasoning the meat with a zesty herb rub before browning. Here is a good example of layering flavors: The fresh tarragon in the pan sauce echoes the flavor of the dried tarragon in the herb rub to create complexity in the finished dish. The creamy mushroom sauce mingles with the pan juices, and is further enhanced by an addition of tangy mustard.

1 Prepare the meat
If you need help trimming a tenderloin, turn to page 39. Trim all the fat and silver skin from the meat. Then, cut the meat into slices about ¼ inch (6 mm) thick. Cut the slices in half.

2 Coat the meat with the mustard-herb rub
In a small bowl, mix together the tarragon, dry mustard, onion powder, salt, and pepper. Rub the mixture all over the meat slices, coating them lightly and evenly. Put the meat on a plate and let stand at room temperature for 30–60 minutes before cooking.

3 Brown the meat and cook the noodles
For more details on browning meat, turn to page 37. Preheat the oven to 200°F (95°C) and put individual plates in the oven to warm. Bring a large pot three-fourths full of salted water to a boil. Place a large frying pan over high heat. When hot, add the olive oil and heat until the surface appears to shimmer. Add the beef slices and cook until lightly browned on one side, about 1 minute. Using tongs, turn over the beef slices and cook the other side until lightly browned, about 30 seconds. The meat will still be rare. Transfer the meat to a plate and cover with aluminum foil to keep warm. Add the noodles to the boiling salted water and cook according to the package directions.

4 Make the sauce
Meanwhile, reduce the heat under the frying pan to medium-high and add the olive oil and butter. When the butter has melted and the foam begins to subside, add the mushrooms, onion, and tarragon and cook, stirring often, until the mushrooms and onion begin to brown, 3–4 minutes. Raise the heat to high, add the stock, and cook, stirring often, until the liquid is reduced by half, 3–5 minutes. Take the pan off the heat and whisk in the sweet mustard and sour cream. Add the Worcestershire sauce, salt, and pepper. Taste the sauce; it should be creamy and slightly tangy. If it tastes a little flat, add a bit more salt or pepper to perk up the flavors. Add the meat and any accumulated juices to the sauce, stir, and reheat gently over medium-low heat for 1–2 minutes.

5 Serve the dish
Drain the noodles, then divide them among the warmed plates. Spoon the meat and sauce over the noodles and sprinkle with the parsley. Serve right away.

5

Grilled
Beef & Veal

Becoming proficient at grilling, like mastering any new skill, takes patience and practice. Along with teaching how to set up a grill, this chapter explains in detail how to season and prepare a variety of tender beef and veal cuts and then grill them to perfection. You will also learn how to use both an instant-read thermometer and a visual cue to determine when steaks or chops are done to your liking.

T-Bone Steaks with Black Olive Butter

Steaks cut from the steer's short loin section, such as T-bones, are naturally tender and juicy and need little adornment. Here, they are seasoned simply with salt and pepper then finished with a compound butter of olives, herbs, and garlic, which complements the flavor of the beef without masking it.

1 Trim and score the steaks

To find out more about trimming and scoring steaks, turn to page 38. Using a rigid boning knife or chef's knife, trim away and discard most of the external fat, leaving a ¼–½-inch (6–12-mm) layer around the edges. Cut 2 or 3 shallow slashes in the fat on each steak to prevent the steaks from curling; this is called *scoring*. Put the steaks in a single layer on a large plate.

2 Season the meat

Sprinkle the steaks evenly on both sides with the salt and pepper, then let them stand at room temperature for 30–60 minutes before grilling. Seasoning the meat this long in advance of cooking helps the seasonings to flavor the meat more fully and enhance the meat's natural juiciness. It is important, too, to bring the meat to room temperature to ensure even cooking.

3 Pit and chop the olives

Spread the olives in a single layer on a cutting board. Lay the flat side of a chef's knife on top of the olives and, applying pressure with your hand, crush them gently. This will cause the olive flesh to split. Use your finger to remove the pits from the olives and discard the pits. Using a rocking motion, run the knife through the olives several times, stopping occasionally to clean the blade of the knife, until they are evenly chopped into small, uniform pieces.

4 Mince the garlic

If you need help mincing garlic, turn to page 33. Place the garlic cloves on a cutting board, firmly press against them with the flat side of a chef's knife, and pull away the papery skim. Rock the knife rhythmically over the garlic to mince it. ❯

2 T-bone steaks, 1½–2 inches (4–5 cm) thick and about 1 lb (500 g) each

2 teaspoons salt

1 teaspoon freshly ground pepper

For the black olive butter

⅓ cup (3 oz/90 g) Mediterranean-style black olives such as Kalamata or Niçoise

2 cloves garlic

3 sprigs fresh thyme

½ cup (4 oz/125 g) unsalted butter, at room temperature

Corn oil for preparing the grill

MAKES 4 SERVINGS

CHEF'S TIP

The same steak could be called by a different name depending on where you live. For example, a strip steak could be labeled as a New York, Kansas City, or Delmonico steak. "London Broil" could refer to flank steak or top-sirloin. When in doubt, ask your butcher to help you locate the steak you seek.

5 **Mince the thyme**
If you are new to mincing thyme, see page 34. Pull the thyme leaves from the stems and discard the stems. Using a rocking motion, run a chef's knife through the thyme leaves several times, stopping occasionally to clean the blade of the knife, until the thyme is minced. You need about 1 teaspoon for this recipe.

6 **Make the black olive butter**
In a bowl, combine the butter, olives, garlic, and thyme. Using a rubber spatula, mash and fold the mixture until it is smooth and uniformly mixed.

7 **Shape the black olive butter into a log**
Place a 12-inch (30-cm) square of waxed paper on a work surface and scrape the butter mixture onto the waxed paper. Form a rough strip down the length of the paper, leaving about 1 inch (2.5 cm) uncovered along the long side and about 2 inches (5 cm) uncovered at each end. Roll the paper around the butter, forming an even log as you roll. Twist the paper at the ends of the log in opposite directions to seal; it will look like a large piece of saltwater taffy. Refrigerate the butter log for at least 30 minutes; this will blend the flavors and make the butter easier to slice.

8 **Set up the grill**
If you need help setting up a grill, turn to pages 40–41. About 15 minutes before you start cooking, prepare a covered gas or charcoal grill with 2 areas of medium-high heat and 1 cooler area. Before igniting either grill, lightly rub the grate with a paper towel coated with corn oil. If you are using a gas grill, turn one burner to medium-high and the other to low. For a charcoal grill, ignite the coals using a chimney starter, then spread the coals 2 or 3 layers deep in one-third of the fire bed and 1 or 2 layers deep in another third of the fire bed; leave the remaining third free of coals. Place a platter near the grill to warm from its heat. >

CHEF'S TIP
To test the heat level of the fire in your charcoal grill, hold your palm an inch (2.5 cm) or so above the cooking grate. If you can count to five before you need to pull away your hand, you have a medium-low fire. If you can count only to four, the fire is medium high. And a count only to three means it is a hot fire.

9>>

10

CHEF'S TIP

I use the following easy method to remember the order in which I placed the steaks on the grill: If it is a round grill, I arrange them in a clockwise pattern starting at 12 o'clock. If it is a rectangular grill, I put them in a left-to-right pattern, just like reading a book.

9 Grill the steaks

If you are new to grilling and creating crosshatch grill marks, turn to page 41. When the gas grill has preheated for 10–15 minutes, or the charcoal is glowing brightly with a faint layer of ash, arrange the steaks on the grill grate over the hottest part so that they line up in the same direction. Remember the order in which you put the steaks on the grill, so that you will know which one to turn over first. Leave the steaks undisturbed for 1–1½ minutes to develop good grill marks. Then, use tongs or a spatula to rotate each steak 90 degrees, and continue cooking, undisturbed, for another 1–1½ minutes. Use the spatula or tongs to turn over the steaks, again lining them up in the same direction. You'll see the square-shaped crosshatching that you created by rotating the steaks at 90 degrees. Repeat the cooking and rotating steps to duplicate the crosshatching on the second side of the steaks. Move the steaks to a cooler area of the grill.

10 Test the steaks for doneness

To find out more about testing steaks for doneness, turn to page 42. Insert an instant-read thermometer into the thickest part of the meat away from the bone, or cut into the steak near the bone (if the grill feels too hot, you can move the steaks to a plate for this step). If you like your steaks rare, they should register 120°F (49°C) on the thermometer or be deep red. For medium-rare, wait until they register 130°F (54°C) or are deep pink. I advise you not to cook the steaks past medium-rare, as they tend to dry out and toughen. If the steaks aren't ready, cover the grill and let them cook, undisturbed, for 3–5 minutes longer and test again. When the steaks are done, transfer them to the warmed platter.

11 Let the steaks rest, then serve

Remove the butter log from the refrigerator, unwrap it, and, using a chef's knife, cut 4 slices ¼ inch (6 mm) thick from the log. Top each steak with 2 butter slices, which will melt and mingle with the meat juices to form a sauce. Loosely cover the steaks with aluminum foil and let them stand for 5 minutes. Carve the steaks (see opposite page) and serve with the butter-laced juices spooned on top.

Carving short-loin steaks

Short-loin steaks, such as T-bones or porter-houses, are about 2 inches (5 cm) thick and have more than enough meat to serve two. Instead of putting a bone-in steak on plates and letting diners cut it themselves, carve the steak first and serve it on individual plates. Not only does carving make a more sophisticated presentation, but it also gives your guests a chance to try a little meat from both the tenderloin and the strip.

Remove the tenderloin portion (top left)
After the steaks have rested, use a carving knife or rigid boning knife to cut the smaller piece of meat (the tenderloin, which is sometimes referred to as the *filet*) away from the bone.

Remove the strip portion (left)
Next, run the knife along the bone to remove the larger piece of meat. This is often called the *strip* and it comes from the top loin part of the steer's short loin.

Cut the steak into slices (above)
Cut each piece into slices ¼ inch (6 mm) thick, then serve the meat, giving diners some of both the tenderloin and the strip. Spoon the butter and any juices from the platter over the meat.

T-Bone Steak Variations

Now that you've mastered T-Bone Steaks with Black Olive Butter (page 91), you know how to set up your gas or charcoal grill, how to create attractive crosshatching, and how to successfully cook steaks. These variations offer six ways to apply this newfound grilling knowledge. Most of them feature an herb or spice mixture for seasoning, while others include instructions for making a simple sauce. Even though some of the recipes call for porterhouse steaks, which have a bigger filet portion than a T-bone, or veal loin chops, which come from a younger animal, the cooking and carving methods that you learned on pages 94–95 are the same. Each variation makes 4 servings.

Florentine-Style Steaks

This classic Italian dish, known as *bistecca alla fiorentina*, is traditionally served with sautéed spinach flavored with lemon juice.

Trim and score 2 porterhouse steaks, 1½–2 inches (4–5 cm) thick and about 1 lb (500 g) each, and place on a plate. In a small bowl, combine 2 minced garlic cloves, 1 tablespoon chopped fresh rosemary, 2 teaspoons kosher salt, 1 teaspoon coarsely ground pepper, and the finely chopped zest and juice of 1 lemon. Stir in 1 tablespoon extra-virgin olive oil to form a thick paste. Rub the paste on all sides of the steaks. Cover the steaks loosely with plastic wrap and let stand at room temperature for 30–60 minutes.

Prepare a medium-hot fire in a gas or charcoal grill. Grill the steaks until done to your liking, 2–3 minutes per side for medium-rare. Let rest for 5 minutes, then carve and serve.

Veal Chops with Lemon & Sage

These juicy grilled veal chops are wonderful accompanied by a simple risotto with butter and cheese.

Trim and score 4 veal loin chops, 1½–2 inches (4–5 cm) thick and about ½ lb (250 g) each, and place on a plate. In a small bowl, combine ¼ cup (⅓ oz/ 10 g) chopped fresh sage, 4 minced garlic cloves, 1 tablespoon salt, 1 tablespoon minced lemon zest, the juice of 1 lemon, and ½ teaspoon lemon pepper. Stir in 1 tablespoon extra-virgin olive oil to form a thick paste. Rub the paste on all sides of the veal chops. Cover the chops loosely with plastic wrap and let stand at room temperature for 30–60 minutes.

Prepare a medium-hot fire in a gas or charcoal grill. Grill the chops until done to your liking, 6–8 minutes per side for medium. Let the chops rest for 5 minutes, then serve 1 whole chop per person.

Chile-Rubbed T-Bone Steaks

T-bones have so much natural flavor that a simple spice rub is the only adornment you need.

Trim and score 2 T-bone steaks, 1½–2 inches (4–5 cm) thick and about 1 lb (500 g) each, and place on a plate. In a small bowl, combine 3 tablespoons pure chile powder, 2 tablespoons garlic powder, 1 tablespoon dried oregano, 2 teaspoons salt, 1 teaspoon ground cumin, and ¼ teaspoon cayenne pepper, or more to taste. Rub the mixture on all sides of the steaks. Cover the steaks loosely with plastic wrap and let stand at room temperature for 30–60 minutes.

Prepare a medium-hot fire in a gas or charcoal grill. Grill the steaks until done to your liking, 2–3 minutes per side for medium-rare. Let rest for 5 minutes, then carve and serve.

Porterhouse Steaks with Sautéed Mushrooms

Fresh mushrooms quickly sautéed with sage and garlic are natural partners for a robust porterhouse.

Trim and score 2 porterhouse steaks, 1½–2 inches (4–5 cm) thick and about 1 lb (500 g) each, and place on a plate. In a small bowl, combine 2 teaspoons dried sage, 2 teaspoons salt, and 1 teaspoon freshly ground pepper. Rub the herb mixture on all sides of the steaks. Cover the steaks loosely with plastic wrap and let stand at room temperature for 30–60 minutes.

Prepare a medium-hot fire in a gas or charcoal grill. Grill the steaks until done to your liking, 2–3 minutes per side for medium-rare. Let rest for 5 minutes.

While the steaks are resting, in a large frying pan over medium-high heat, warm 2 tablespoons olive oil. Add 1 lb (500 g) chopped fresh mushrooms (shiitake, morel, chanterelle, or a mixture), 4 minced shallots, 4 minced garlic cloves, and 2 teaspoons chopped fresh sage and sauté until the mushrooms are lightly browned, 4–6 minutes. Add ¼ cup (2 fl oz/60 ml) Madeira and ¼ cup (2 fl oz/60 ml) Roasted Meat Stock (page 20) and cook, stirring often, until reduced by half, 2–3 minutes. Add 1 teaspoon salt and ½ teaspoon freshly ground pepper. Adjust the seasonings. Remove from the heat and swirl in 2 tablespoons unsalted butter and ¼ cup (⅓ oz/10 g) chopped fresh flat-leaf (Italian) parsley.

Carve the steaks, then spoon the mushrooms alongside each serving.

Tuscan-Style Veal Chops

The fresh and hearty tomato sauce brings out the delicate flavors of the veal in this recipe from the hills of Tuscany.

Make 1 batch Roasted Tomato Sauce (page 26) and set aside. Next, trim and score 4 veal loin chops, 1½–2 inches (4–5 cm) thick and about ½ lb (250 g) each, and place on a plate. Season both sides of the chops with ½ teaspoon salt and ½ teaspoon freshly ground pepper, dividing evenly. Cover the chops loosely with plastic wrap and let stand at room temperature for 30–60 minutes.

Prepare a medium-hot fire in a gas or charcoal grill. Grill the chops until done to your liking, 6–8 minutes per side for medium. Let the chops rest for 5 minutes.

While the chops are resting, warm the tomato sauce over medium heat until heated through. Serve 1 whole chop per person. Top each chop with a large spoonful of sauce.

Veal Chops Stuffed with Roasted Red Peppers

This aromatic stuffing flavors veal chops from the inside.

Trim and score 4 veal loin chops, 1½–2 inches (4–5 cm) thick and about ½ lb (250 g) each, and place on a plate. In a small bowl, combine ¼ cup (2 oz/60 g) chopped roasted red peppers (capsicums), 2 tablespoons chopped fresh thyme, 2 finely chopped large garlic cloves, ¼ teaspoon salt, and ¼ teaspoon freshly ground pepper. Cover the chops loosely with plastic wrap and let stand at room temperature for 30–60 minutes.

Starting on the side of the chop away from the bone, use a paring knife to cut a deep, wide, horizontal pocket into each chop. Cut all the way to the bone, but take care not to cut through the top or bottom of the chop. Using a spoon or your fingers, insert about 1 tablespoon of the red pepper mixture into each pocket, then secure each pocket with a toothpick. Season both sides of the chops with ½ teaspoon salt and ½ teaspoon freshly ground pepper, dividing evenly.

Prepare a medium-hot fire in a gas or charcoal grill. Grill the chops until done to your liking, 6–8 minutes per side for medium. Let the chops rest for 5 minutes, then remove the toothpicks. Serve 1 whole chop per person.

Soy-Marinated Skirt Steak or Flank Steak

Flank steaks and skirt steaks are terrific on the grill, where the smoke complements their robust flavor. Relatively thin, these moderately tender steaks cut from the belly of the steer are often further tenderized with a marinade, such as this full-flavored, Asian-inspired mixture. Cutting them across the grain also ensures a tender texture.

1 Prepare the meat

Lay the skirt steak or flank steak on a cutting board and notice which way the meat fibers are running—this is called the *grain*. The skirt steak can be very long, so cut it into 3 or 4 equal pieces; this will make the meat easier to handle. Using a rigid boning knife or a chef's knife, make 2 or 3 evenly spaced shallow cuts over the surface of each piece of meat in the opposite direction of the meat fibers— or, across the grain. Turn the meat over and repeat the cutting on the opposite side. This technique, called *scoring*, will prevent the steak from curling as it cooks.

2 Mince the garlic and ginger for the marinade

If you are new to mincing garlic and ginger, turn to pages 33 and 36. First, mince the garlic: Place the garlic cloves on a work surface, firmly press against them with the flat side of a chef's knife, and pull away the papery skin. Rock the knife rhythmically over the garlic to mince it. Next, mince the ginger: Using a vegetable peeler, remove the thin beige skin from the ginger, and then use the chef's knife to cut it into coin-shaped slices, then strips. Cut the strips into small pieces, then mince. Measure out 1½ tablespoons.

3 Marinate the beef

In a shallow glass or ceramic dish, stir together the soy sauce, rice vinegar, orange juice, honey, sesame oil, chile oil, garlic, and ginger. Add the meat to the dish and turn the meat in the marinade to make sure it is completely coated. Let the meat marinate at room temperature for at least 30 minutes and up to 1 hour, turning occasionally with tongs to help the marinade penetrate the meat evenly. You don't want to marinate the steaks for too long, as the soy sauce, vinegar, and citrus juice can break down the fibers of the meat, resulting in a mushy texture.

4 Set up the grill

If you need help setting up a grill, turn to pages 40–41. About 15 minutes before you plan to start cooking, prepare a covered gas or charcoal grill with 2 areas of medium-high heat and 1 cooler area. Before igniting either grill, lightly rub the grate with a paper towel coated with corn oil. If you are using a gas grill, turn one burner to medium-high and the other to low. For a charcoal grill, ignite the coals using a chimney starter, then spread the coals 2 or 3 layers deep in one-third of the fire bed, 1 or 2 layers deep in another third of the fire bed, and leave the remaining third free of coals. Place a platter near the grill to warm from its heat. ⟩

1 skirt steak or flank steak, 2–2½ lb (1–1.25 kg), trimmed of all fat (page 38)

For the marinade

6 cloves garlic

2-inch (5-cm) piece fresh ginger

¼ cup (2 fl oz/60 ml) reduced-sodium soy sauce

2 tablespoons rice vinegar

¼ cup (2 fl oz/60 ml) fresh orange juice

1 teaspoon honey

1 tablespoon Asian sesame oil

1 or 2 dashes Asian chile oil

Corn oil for preparing the grill

MAKES 4 SERVINGS

CHEF'S TIP

Always slice flank and skirt steaks across the grain to enhance their tenderness. The grain on the skirt steak will vary slightly down its length. You may need to change the angle of your knife as you progress.

5 Grill the steak

Take the meat out of the marinade and pat it dry with paper towels. Removing the extra moisture from the surface of the meat before grilling will ensure that it will brown nicely on the surface. If you are new to grilling and creating crosshatch grill marks, turn to page 41. When the gas grill has preheated for 10–15 minutes, or the charcoal is glowing brightly with a faint layer of ash, arrange the steak on the grill grate over the hottest part. If you have cut the meat into pieces, make sure the pieces are lined up in the same direction. Cook for 2–3 minutes, using tongs or a spatula to rotate the meat 90 degrees about halfway through (this will create attractive crosshatching). Turn the meat over and repeat the cooking and rotating steps to mark the other side. Move the meat to the cooler area of the grill. If at any time during grilling you notice charring on the exterior—caused by the sugary marinade—move the meat to a cooler area of the grill to finish cooking; the timing will be slightly longer.

6 Test the steak for doneness

To find out more about testing steaks for doneness, turn to page 42. Insert an instant-read thermometer into the thickest part of the meat, or cut into the center (if the grill feels too hot, you can move the steaks to a plate for this step). If you like your steak rare, it should register 120°F (49°C) on the thermometer or be deep red. If you prefer your steak medium-rare, wait until it registers 130°F (54°C) or is deep pink. I advise you not to cook the steaks past medium-rare, as they tend to dry out and toughen. If the steaks aren't ready, cover the grill and let them cook, undisturbed, for 3–5 minutes longer, and test again.

7 Let the steak rest

Use the tongs or spatula to transfer the steaks to the warmed platter. Cover the steaks loosely with aluminum foil and let stand for 5 minutes. This resting period gives the meat's juices, which rise to the surface during cooking, an opportunity to settle and redistribute themselves throughout the meat. The temperature will rise about 5°F (3°C) while the steaks rest.

8 Serve the steak

After resting, transfer the steaks to a carving board and, using a carving knife or chef's knife, cut the steak across the grain on the diagonal into slices ¼–½ inch (6–12 mm) thick. Serve right away.

Marinated Skirt Steak or Flank Steak Variations

As you learned in the master recipe for Soy-Marinated Skirt Steak or Flank Steak on page 99, a marinade that includes an acidic ingredient such as citrus juice or wine helps break down the meat's connective tissues, contributing to tender, juicy meat. Marinades are also a wonderful way to infuse the beef with flavor. In one variation, a bourbon–soy sauce marinade is spiced up with chiles, and another pairs a red-wine marinade with slowly caramelized onions. The last one details how to make a traditional Argentinian vinaigrette flavored with parsley and cilantro, which is used as both a marinade and a sauce. Each variation makes 4 servings.

Bourbon-Marinated Flank Steak

Bourbon, a popular ingredient in Southern-style cooking, makes a potent marniade that complements the chewy steaks.

Follow the recipe for Soy-Marinated Skirt Steak or Flank Steak, replacing the marinade with the one that follows.

To make the bourbon marinade, in a shallow glass dish, combine ¼ cup (2 fl oz/60 ml) bourbon whiskey, ¼ cup (2 fl oz/60 ml) reduced-sodium soy sauce, ¼ cup (2 fl oz/ 60 ml) olive oil, 1 seeded and finely chopped serrano chile, 1 seeded and finely chopped Anaheim chile, 1 chopped yellow onion, and 2 chopped garlic cloves.

Wine-Marinated Flank Steak with Red Onion Jam

Thick red-onion jam dresses up this red wine–marinated flank steak.

In a large frying pan over medium heat, melt ½ cup (4 oz/125 g) unsalted butter. Stir in 4 thinly sliced large red onions, reduce the heat to low, and sauté until the onions are the color of light milk chocolate, 45–60 minutes. Increase the heat to medium-high and deglaze with ¼ cup (2 fl oz/60 ml) dry red wine such as Zinfandel. Cook, stirring often, until the pan is almost dry, 5–8 minutes. Off the heat, stir in 1 tablespoon honey, 1 teaspoon salt, and ½ teaspoon freshly ground pepper. Set aside.

Next, follow the recipe for Soy-Marinated Skirt Steak or Flank Steak, replacing the marinade with the one that follows.

To make the red wine marinade, in a shallow glass dish, combine ½ cup (4 fl oz/ 125 ml) Zinfandel, ¼ cup (2 fl oz/60 ml) olive oil, ¼ cup (2 fl oz/60 ml) red wine vinegar, 1 sliced yellow onion, 4 minced garlic cloves, 2 bay leaves, 2 teaspoons salt, and 1 teaspoon freshly ground pepper.

Serve the carved steak with the onion jam on the side.

Skirt Steak or Flank Steak with Chimichurri

In Argentina, the classic marinade and condiment *chimichurri* is used with a wide variety of grilled and roasted meats.

Follow the recipe for Soy-Marinated Skirt Steak or Flank Steak, replacing the marinade with the one that follows.

To make the *chimichurri*, in the bowl of a food processor, combine 1½ cups (2¼ oz/65 g) chopped fresh flat-leaf (Italian) parsley, 1 cup (1½ oz/45 g) chopped fresh cilantro (fresh coriander), 8 peeled garlic cloves, ½ cup (4 fl oz/ 125 ml) extra-virgin olive oil, ¼ cup (2 fl oz/ 60 ml) red wine vinegar, 2 teaspoons salt, and 1 teaspoon freshly ground pepper. Process until well blended but not smooth. Pour half into a glass bowl and set aside. Next, pour the other half over the meat, cover, and refrigerate for 2–4 hours to marinate. Let the meat come to room temperature before grilling, about 30 minutes.

Serve the carved steak with the reserved *chimichurri*.

Boneless Steaks with Gorgonzola Butter

Boneless steaks from the rib, loin, or tenderloin are tender and full of great beef flavor. They're not as expensive as T-bone and porterhouse steaks, but like these cuts they only need a simple flavoring such as this pungent compound butter made from Gorgonzola cheese and roasted garlic paste.

4 boneless strip steaks or rib-eye steaks, at least 1½ inches (4 cm) thick and ½–¾ lb (250–375 g) each

1 tablespoon extra-virgin olive oil

2 teaspoons salt

1 teaspoon freshly ground pepper

For the Gorgonzola butter

½ cup (4 oz/125 g) unsalted butter, at room temperature

2 tablespoons crumbled Gorgonzola cheese

2 teaspoons roasted garlic paste (see Chef's Tip below)

2 teaspoons dried thyme

½ teaspoon salt

Corn oil for preparing the grill

MAKES 4 SERVINGS

CHEF'S TIP
Roasted garlic paste can be used alone or as a condiment for grilled or roasted beef, or it can be combined with other ingredients. Cut the top from 1 garlic head, place in a small baking pan, and drizzle with 1 tablespoon olive oil. Then, cover with aluminum foil and roast at 425°F (220°C) until soft, about 45 minutes. When cool, squeeze the pulp from the skin and mash with a fork.

1 **Trim and season the steaks**
If you are not sure how to trim steaks, turn to page 38. Trim the steaks, leaving ¼ inch (6 mm) of fat on the edges. Cut 2 or 3 shallow slashes in the fat on each steak. (If using rib-eye steaks, cut out the nugget of fat in the center.) Put the steaks on a plate, brush with the olive oil, and sprinkle with the salt and pepper, dividing evenly. Let stand at room temperature for 30–60 minutes before grilling.

2 **Make the Gorgonzola butter**
In a bowl, combine the butter, cheese, roasted garlic paste, thyme, and salt. Using a rubber spatula, mash the mixture until smooth. Scrape the mixture into a rough strip down the length of a 12-inch (30-cm) square of waxed paper, leaving a 1–2-inch (2.5–5-cm) border, and roll it into a tight log. Twist the paper at the ends of the log to seal, and refrigerate for at least 30 minutes.

3 **Grill the steaks**
For details on cooking with a grill, turn to page 40. About 15 minutes before you start cooking, prepare a covered gas or charcoal grill with 2 areas of medium-high heat and 1 cooler area. Place a platter near the grill to warm. Before igniting either grill, lightly rub the grate with a paper towel coated with corn oil. When the gas grill has preheated for 10–15 minutes, or the charcoal is glowing brightly with a faint layer of ash, arrange the steaks on the grill grate over the hottest part so that they line up in the same direction. Cook for 2–3 minutes, using tongs to rotate them 90 degrees about halfway through. Turn over the steaks and repeat the cooking and rotating steps. Move the steaks to a cooler area of the grill.

4 **Test the steaks for doneness and let them rest**
If you are not sure how to check steaks for doneness, turn to page 42. Insert an instant-read thermometer into the thickest part of the meat, or cut into the center. If you like your steaks rare, they should register 120°F (49°C) or be deep red. For medium-rare, wait until they register 130°F (54°C) or are deep pink. If the steaks aren't ready, cover the grill and let them cook, undisturbed, for 3–5 minutes longer and test again. Transfer the steaks to the warmed platter and let them rest, loosely covered with aluminum foil, for about 5 minutes.

5 **Serve the steaks**
Unwrap the butter, then use a chef's knife to cut 4 slices ½ inch (12 mm) thick from the log. Top each steak with a slice and serve right away.

Bacon-Wrapped Filets Mignons

Wrapping bacon around filets mignons—steaks cut from the narrow end of the tenderloin—is an example of the classic French technique called *barding*. Covering lean pieces of meat such as these with bacon slices or thin sheets of pork fat contributes flavor and moisture to the finished dish. I further enhance this special-occasion steak with earthy truffle-infused olive oil.

1 Trim and season the meat

If you need help trimming filets mignons, turn to page 39. Trim all the fat and silver skin from the meat. Rub the meat on all sides with the 2 tablespoons truffle oil and sprinkle with the salt and pepper. Put the meat on a plate and let stand at room temperature for 30–60 minutes before grilling.

2 Wrap the steaks with bacon

Preheat the oven broiler (grill). Lay the bacon slices in a single layer on a rimmed baking sheet. Cook the bacon under the broiler until lightly browned but still pliable, 5–7 minutes. Using tongs or a fork, transfer the bacon to a plate lined with paper towels and set aside. When cool enough to handle, wrap 2 strips of bacon around each filet mignon and tie them securely with kitchen string.

3 Grill the steaks

If you need help setting up and cooking with a grill, turn to pages 40–41. About 15 minutes before you start cooking, prepare a covered gas or charcoal grill with 2 areas of medium-high heat and 1 cooler area. Place a platter near the grill to warm from its heat. Before igniting either grill, lightly rub the grate with a paper towel coated with corn oil. When the gas grill has preheated for 10–15 minutes, or the charcoal is glowing brightly with a faint layer of ash, arrange the steaks on the grill grate over the hottest part so that they line up in the same direction. Cook for 2–3 minutes, using tongs to rotate them 90 degrees about halfway through. Turn over the steaks and repeat the cooking and rotating steps on the other side. Move the steaks to the cooler area of the grill.

4 Test the steaks for doneness and let them rest

If you are not sure how to check steaks for doneness, turn to page 42. Insert an instant-read thermometer into the thickest part of the meat, or cut into the center. If you like your steaks rare, they should register 120°F (49°C) or be deep red. For medium-rare, wait until they register 130°F (54°C) or are deep pink. If the steaks aren't ready, cover the grill and let them cook, undisturbed, for 3–5 minutes longer and test again. Transfer the steaks to the warmed platter and let them rest, loosely covered with aluminum foil, for about 5 minutes.

5 Serve the steaks

Using kitchen scissors or a knife, cut off the string and discard it; the crisp, cooked bacon will hold its shape on the meat. Drizzle each steak with a little truffle oil and serve right away.

4 filets mignons, at least 2 inches (5 cm) thick and 6–8 ounces (185–250 g) each

2 tablespoons white or black truffle oil, plus extra for drizzling over the steaks

1 teaspoon salt

1 teaspoon freshly ground pepper

8 slices thick-cut lightly smoked bacon

Corn oil for preparing the grill

MAKES 4 SERVINGS

CHEF'S TIP
Professional chefs can tell when a steak is done by poking it with a fingertip and evaluating its firmness. If it feels soft, the meat is rare. If your touch meets with a little resistance but springs back, it is medium-rare. If it feels firm and has no spring, it is well done.

Beef Ribs with Barbecue Sauce

Many recipes for beef ribs grill them as a rack and cut them up before serving, but some cooks like to cut the racks into ribs and grill them individually to make them extra crispy. The mildly hot spice mixture rubbed on the ribs complements the tangy barbecue-style sauce that I use to coat them near the end of grilling.

6 lb (3 kg) beef ribs, in racks or separated into ribs by the butcher

For the rub

4 tablespoons hot or sweet paprika, or a mixture

2 tablespoons chili powder

1 tablespoon dry mustard

1 tablespoon garlic powder

1 tablespoon ground cumin

1 tablespoon dried sage

1 tablespoon salt

1 tablespoon freshly ground black pepper

For the barbecue sauce

1 cup (8 fl oz/250 ml) Basic Tomato Sauce (page 24) or purchased tomato sauce

1 cup (8 fl oz/250 ml) tomato ketchup

½ cup (4 oz/125 g) horseradish mustard or other spicy mustard

¼ cup (2 oz/60 g) firmly packed golden brown sugar

¼ cup (2 fl oz/60 ml) cider vinegar

4 cloves garlic, finely chopped (page 33)

1 tablespoon Worcestershire sauce

½ teaspoon cayenne pepper

1 teaspoon salt

Corn oil for preparing the grill

MAKES 4–6 SERVINGS

1 **Trim and season the ribs**
If you purchased your ribs in racks, use a chef's knife to cut between the bones and separate the rack into individual ribs. Resist the urge to trim the fat from the ribs; it keeps the ribs moist and flavorful during cooking. Next, make the spice rub: In a small bowl, mix together the paprika, chili powder, dry mustard, garlic powder, cumin, sage, salt, and black pepper. Rub the ribs thoroughly with the mixture until they are evenly coated. Put the ribs on a plate and let stand at room temperature for 30–60 minutes before grilling.

2 **Make the barbecue sauce**
In a heavy-bottomed saucepan over medium-low heat, stir together the tomato sauce, ketchup, horseradish mustard, brown sugar, vinegar, garlic, Worcestershire sauce, and cayenne pepper. Cook, stirring often, until the sauce has reduced slightly, about 30 minutes. Stir in the salt, then taste the sauce. If you feel the sauce tastes dull, add a little more salt or cayenne until the flavor is to your liking. Remove the sauce from the heat.

3 **Grill the ribs**
If you need help setting up a grill for indirect grilling, turn to page 40. About 15 minutes before you start cooking, prepare a covered gas or charcoal grill with 1 or 2 areas of medium-high heat and 1 area with no heat. (If using charcoal, place a drip pan in the unheated area.) Place a platter near the grill to warm from the heat of the grill. Before igniting either grill, lightly rub the grate with a paper towel coated with corn oil. When the gas grill has preheated for 10–15 minutes, or the charcoal is glowing brightly with a faint layer of ash, put the ribs over the hottest part of the grill. Cook the ribs, using tongs to turn them often, until well browned on all sides, 3–5 minutes total. Move the ribs to the unheated portion of the grill and use a brush to coat them liberally with the barbecue sauce. Cover the grill and cook the ribs, turning and basting with sauce about every 5 minutes, until they are crisp and tender, 12–15 minutes. To test the ribs for doneness, cut into one with a paring knife; it should slip through easily, and the interior should have no trace of pink. If the ribs are not ready, cover the grill and let them cook, undisturbed, for 5–7 minutes longer and test again.

4 **Serve the ribs**
Return the barbecue sauce to medium heat and let simmer for at least 5 minutes. Heap the ribs on the warmed platter and serve right away, passing the heated barbecue sauce at the table.

Braised
Beef & Veal

In this chapter, you'll learn how to *braise*, or cook tougher beef and veal cuts—chuck, short ribs, shank—in a moderate amount of flavorful liquid until they are fork-tender. Braises and stews are closely related, although stews are made with more liquid and don't cook as long. These recipes will also show you how to thicken the meat-infused braising liquids, turning them into delicious sauces.

Beef Bourguignonne

My recipe for this classic French dish of beef braised in dry red wine features the usual ingredients—bacon, pearl onions, and mushrooms. But I like to coat the cubes of beef chuck with a dried thyme rub before browning them. A second addition of thyme, to the braising liquid, reinforces the flavor.

1 Make the herb rub and bouquet garni

In a small bowl, mix together the dried thyme, salt, and pepper. Set aside. If you are not sure how to make a bouquet garni, turn to page 37. Trim the top 4 inches (10 cm) of the celery stalk to use in the bouquet garni, and save the rest for another use. Wrap the parsley sprigs, thyme sprigs, bay leaf, and celery in a piece of damp cheesecloth (muslin) and secure with kitchen string. Set aside.

2 Prepare the meat

To find out more about trimming meat, turn to page 38. Using a chef's knife or a rigid boning knife, trim away and discard most of the external fat from the chuck, leaving ¼–½ inch (6–12 mm) on the exterior of the meat. Then, cut the beef into 2-inch (5-cm) chunks.

3 Season the meat

Put the beef chunks in a large glass bowl. Sprinkle the herb rub over the meat and then toss the pieces so that they are evenly coated. Cover the bowl and let the meat stand at room temperature for at least 30 minutes or up to 1 hour so that the meat has time to absorb the flavors. Allowing the meat to come to room temperature also encourages even cooking.

4 Prepare the vegetables

To find out more about preparing the onion and garlic, turn to pages 32 and 33. First, dice the onion: Cut the onion in half lengthwise and peel each half. One at a time, place the onion halves, cut side down, on a cutting board. Alternately make a series of lengthwise cuts, parallel cuts, and then crosswise cuts to create ¼-inch (6-mm) dice. Be sure to stop just short of the root end; this holds the onion together as you cut. Next, mince the garlic: Place the garlic cloves on a work surface, firmly press against them with the flat side of a chef's knife, and pull away the papery skin. Rock the knife rhythmically over the garlic to mince it. Finally, peel and slice the carrots: Using a vegetable peeler, peel the carrots. Then, using the chef's knife, cut the carrots into 1-inch (2.5-cm) pieces on the diagonal.

5 Cut the bacon

Using a chef's knife, cut the bacon crosswise into strips ½ inch (12 mm) wide. These strips of bacon resemble the French *lardons*, which are small strips of fat taken from the belly of a pig. *Lardons* are a common addition to many country-style French dishes. ❯

For the rub

1 tablespoon dried thyme

1 teaspoon salt

½ teaspoon freshly ground pepper

For the bouquet garni

1 stalk celery with leaves

3 sprigs fresh flat-leaf (Italian) parsley

3 sprigs fresh thyme

1 bay leaf

2 lb (1 kg) boneless beef chuck

1 yellow onion

2 cloves garlic

3 carrots

3 slices thick-cut lightly smoked bacon

1 tablespoon corn oil

1–2 cups (8–16 fl oz/250–500 ml) Roasted Meat Stock (page 20)

1½ cups (12 fl oz/375 ml) dry red wine such as Zinfandel

12 pearl onions

12 small fresh white or brown mushrooms

1 tablespoon extra-virgin olive oil

1 teaspoon salt

½ teaspoon freshly ground pepper

1½ teaspoons cornstarch (cornflour), if needed to thicken the sauce

6 sprigs fresh flat-leaf (Italian) parsley

MAKES 4 SERVINGS

Browning the beef chunks in the bacon fat infuses them with smoky flavor. This flavor is repeated with the addition of the strips of crisply fried bacon later in the recipe.

7

8

To test braised dishes for doneness, insert the tines of a fork into the meat. If it slips in and out easily, you'll know the meat is done without needing to use a thermometer.

6 Cook the bacon

Put an oven rack in the middle of the oven and preheat to 350°F (180°C). Place a large Dutch oven over medium-high heat. When it's hot (you'll be able to feel the heat rising upward when you hold your hand over the pot), add the corn oil and heat until the surface appears to shimmer. Add the bacon and cook, stirring constantly, until the bacon pieces are browned and crisp, 3–5 minutes. Using a slotted spoon, transfer the bacon to a plate lined with a paper towel to drain. Carefully pour off all but 2 tablespoons of the fat and save it for another use or discard. (Don't pour the fat down the drain, as it can cause clogs.)

7 Brown the meat

For more details on browning meat, turn to page 37. Using tongs, add just enough beef pieces to the remaining hot fat in the pot to form a single layer. Do not crowd the beef or it will steam, rather than brown (you may need to brown it in 2 batches). Cook over medium-high heat, turning the pieces often, until all surfaces are browned, about 5 minutes total. Browning, or *searing*, meat caramelizes the surface, resulting in a richer flavor and an appetizing appearance. Using a large metal spoon, transfer the meat to a plate.

8 Cook the vegetables and deglaze the pot

Add the onion, garlic, and carrots to the the pot. Cook over medium-high heat, stirring often, until the onions are lightly browned, 3–5 minutes. Browning the vegetables caramelizes the surface, enhancing their natural sweetness. Pour 1 cup (8 fl oz/250 ml) of the stock and the wine into the pot and bring to a boil over high heat, scraping up the browned bits on the bottom and sides of the pot with a wooden spoon. These browned bits, or *fond*, will also add good flavor to the final sauce. For more details on deglazing, turn to page 43.

9 Braise the meat

Add the bouquet garni to the pot along with the browned meat chunks, the juices from the plate, and the cooked bacon. The liquid should come three-fourths of the way up the sides of the meat; if it doesn't, supplement it with more stock. Cover the pot, put it in the oven, and let it cook, undisturbed, in the steady heat of the oven. After 1½ hours, use oven mitts to carefully pull the pot out of the oven. Uncover the pot and insert the tines of a fork into the meat; if the fork slips in and out with little resistance, the meat is done. (Braised meat becomes tender at the well-done stage, so you won't need a thermometer.) If the meat is not ready, re-cover the pot, return it to the oven, and continue to cook, testing the meat every 15 minutes. The total braising time may be up to 3 hours.

10 Defat the braising liquid

When the meat is done, remove the pot from the oven and let it cool for about 10 minutes. If time allows, let the meat and sauce cool to room temperature, then cover and refrigerate overnight. The next day the fat can be easily lifted off the surface of the stew and the flavors will be fully developed. To serve the dish right away, use a large metal spoon to skim the fat from the surface.

11 Prepare the pearl onions and mushrooms

Use a paring knife to trim off the root ends of the onions. Fill a saucepan three-fourths full of water and bring to a boil over high heat. Add the onions and let them partially cook in the rapidly bubbling water for about 4 minutes. Drain, then quickly transfer them to a bowl of cold water to stop the cooking. These processes, known as *blanching* and *shocking,* respectively, will help loosen the skins. Drain the onions again and use your fingers to peel off the skins; they should now pull away easily. Wipe the mushrooms with a damp cloth. Trim the stems flush with the caps and discard the stems.

12 Brown the onions and mushrooms

Place a nonstick frying pan over medium-high heat. When the pan is hot (you'll be able to feel the heat rising upward when you hold your hand over the pan), add the olive oil and heat until the surface appears to shimmer. Add the onions and mushrooms and cook, stirring constantly with a wooden spatula, until lightly browned, 3–5 minutes. Pour the onions and mushrooms into a bowl to stop the cooking. The onions and mushrooms are cooked separately from the rest of the dish to bring out their flavors better.

13 Finish the dish

Preheat the oven to 200°F (95°C) and put individual bowls in the oven to warm. Stir the onions and mushrooms into the pot with the meat and sauce mixture. Put the pot on the stove top over low heat and reheat the mixture gently, stirring from time to time, until it is heated through. If you have refrigerated the dish overnight, this will take about 15 minutes; otherwise, it will take about 5 minutes.

14 Adjust the seasonings and consistency

Stir in the salt and pepper, and taste the sauce. It should taste rich from the stock and red wine and earthy from the herbs and vegetables. If it tastes a little dull, stir in a bit more salt and pepper to perk up the flavors. If the sauce seems too thick, stir in either more wine or stock, 2 tablespoons at a time, until the sauce has a nice spoon-coating consistency. If the sauce seems too thin, make a slurry by whisking together the cornstarch (cornflour) with 2 tablespoons cold stock or wine in a small bowl. (For more details on using a slurry, turn to page 43.) Whisk a little of the slurry into the simmering sauce, then bring to a boil just until the sauce thickens, 1 minute or less. If the sauce is not sufficiently thickened, add a little more of the slurry and boil again.

15 Serve the dish

For more details on mincing parsley, turn to page 35. Pull the leaves from the parsley stems and discard the stems. Rock a knife rhythmically over the leaves to mince them finely. Ladle the beef, vegetables, and sauce into the warmed bowls, dividing evenly, sprinkle with the minced parsley, and serve right away.

Serving ideas

To determine how you want to present and serve this dish, consider both who your guests are and the setting. If you are serving the Beef Bourguignonne at a casual gathering, you might think about transferring the braise to a tureen or soup pot that you can put on the table and cover to keep warm. For plated servings that include bread, potatoes, or noodles on the side, select attractive individual plates or bowls.

Full meal (top left)
Ladling this braise into a deep plate or shallow bowl alongside mashed potatoes is an excellent way to serve a one-dish meal.

Family style (left)
Choose a large tureen that will look attractive on the table and serve from there. Leave the tureen on the table, covered, to keep the braise warm and within easy reach of diners who might want seconds. Remember to provide serving utensils.

Single serving (above)
Sometimes all this dish needs is a hunk of crusty sourdough or sweet baguette to sop up the rich juices that pool in a deep, single-serving bowl.

Beef Bourguignonne Variations

Now that you have learned how to prepare Beef Bourguignonne (page 111), you should feel confident making a bouquet garni, trimming and browning meat, deglazing a pan, and thickening a braising liquid to create a rich and flavorful sauce for serving with the braised meat. Some of these variations, such as Beef Braised in Barbera, Beef Daube, and Beef Carbonnade, are classic regional European braises that use local wines and beers for the braising liquid, while Red-Cooked Beef illustrates how simple it is to capture the flavors of Asian cuisine by changing the herb rub, liquid, and vegetables in the master recipe. Each variation makes 4 servings.

Beef Braised in Barbera

This Italian-style braised beef dish is infused with garlic and oregano.

In a small bowl, mix together 1 tablespoon dried oregano, 1 tablespoon garlic powder, 1 teaspoon salt, and ½ teaspoon freshly ground pepper. Make a bouquet garni by tying a 4-inch (10-cm) piece celery with leaves, 3 sprigs *each* fresh flat-leaf (Italian) parsley and oregano, and 1 bay leaf in dampened cheesecloth (muslin). Sprinkle 2 lb (1 kg) beef chuck pieces (2-inch/5-cm pieces) with the herb rub and let stand for 30–60 minutes.

Preheat the oven to 325°C (165°F). In a Dutch oven, brown the meat in 2 tablespoons olive oil. Add 1 chopped yellow onion, 5 chopped garlic cloves, and 3 peeled and coarsely chopped carrots and sauté until lightly browned, 3–5 minutes. Deglaze the pot with 1 cup (8 fl oz/250 ml) Roasted Meat Stock (page 20) and 2 cups (16 fl oz/500 ml) Barbera or other full-bodied red wine. Stir in 1 cup (8 fl oz/250 ml) Basic Tomato Sauce (page 24) and the bouquet garni.

Braise in the oven until tender, about 3 hours. Defat the sauce. If the sauce is too thin, whisk in 1 tablespoon tomato paste; if too thick, add more wine. Adjust the seasonings and serve right away.

Balsamic-Braised Beef

Balsamic vinegar gives the braising liquid a complex acidity.

In a small bowl, mix together 1 tablespoon dried marjoram, 1 tablespoon garlic powder, 1 teaspoon salt, and ½ teaspoon freshly ground pepper. Make a bouquet garni by tying a 4-inch (10-cm) piece celery with leaves, 3 sprigs *each* fresh flat-leaf (Italian) parsley and thyme, and 1 bay leaf in dampened cheesecloth (muslin). Sprinkle 2 lb (1 kg) beef chuck pieces (2-inch/5-cm pieces) with the herb rub and let stand for 30–60 minutes.

Preheat the oven to 325°C (165°F). In a Dutch oven, brown the meat in 2 tablespoons olive oil. Add 1 diced yellow onion, 6 cloves minced garlic, and 3 peeled and coarsely chopped carrots and sauté until lightly browned, 3–5 minutes. Deglaze the pot with 1½ cups (12 fl oz/ 375 ml) Roasted Meat Stock (page 20), ¼ cup (2 fl oz/60 ml) balsamic vinegar, and 1 cup (8 fl oz/250 ml) dry red wine. Stir in 1 cup (8 fl oz/250 ml) Basic Tomato Sauce (page 24) and the bouquet garni.

Braise in the oven until tender, about 3 hours. Defat the sauce. If the sauce is too thin, whisk in 1 tablespoon tomato paste; if too thick, add more wine. Adjust the seasonings and serve right away.

Garlic-Braised Beef

A generous measure of garlic adds a nutty and flavorful accent to this braise.

In a small bowl, mix together 1 tablespoon dried thyme, 1 tablespoon garlic powder, 1 teaspoon salt, and ½ teaspoon freshly ground pepper. Make a bouquet garni by tying a 4-inch (10-cm) piece celery with leaves, 3 sprigs *each* fresh flat-leaf (Italian) parsley and oregano, and 1 bay leaf in dampened cheesecloth (muslin). Sprinkle 2 lb (1 kg) beef chuck pieces (2-inch/5-cm pieces) with the herb rub and let stand for 30–60 minutes.

Preheat the oven to 325°C (165°F). In a Dutch oven, brown the meat in 2 tablespoons olive oil. Add 1 diced yellow onion, 6 cloves minced garlic, and 3 peeled and coarsely chopped carrots and sauté until lightly browned, 3–5 minutes. Deglaze the pot with 1 cup (8 fl oz/250 ml) Roasted Meat Stock (page 20) and 1½ cups (12 fl oz/375 ml) dry white wine such as Pinot Grigio. Stir in 1 cup (8 fl oz/250 ml) Basic Tomato Sauce (page 24) and the bouquet garni.

Braise in the oven until tender, about 3 hours. Defat the sauce. If the sauce is too thin, whisk in 1 tablespoon tomato paste; if too thick, add more wine. Adjust the seasonings and serve right away.

Beef Daube

In this traditional braise from the Provence region of France, vermouth and orange juice are used for part of the braising liquid.

In a small bowl, mix together 1 tablespoon dried *herbes de Provence,* 2 tablespoons garlic powder, 1 teaspoon salt, and ½ teaspoon freshly ground pepper. Make a bouquet garni by tying a 4-inch (10-cm) piece celery with leaves, 3 sprigs *each* fresh flat-leaf (Italian) parsley and basil, 1 sprig fresh lavender, 1 bay leaf, and 2 strips orange zest (2-by-½-inch/5-cm-by-12-mm strips) in dampened cheesecloth (muslin). Sprinkle 2 lb (1 kg) beef chuck pieces (2-inch/5-cm pieces) with the herb rub and let stand for 30–60 minutes.

Preheat the oven to 325°C (165°F). In a Dutch oven, brown the meat in 2 tablespoons olive oil. Add 1 diced yellow onion, 10 crushed garlic cloves, and 3 peeled and coarsely chopped carrots and sauté until lightly browned, 3–5 minutes. Deglaze the pot with 1½ cups (12 fl oz/ 375 ml) Roasted Meat Stock (page 20), 1 cup (8 fl oz/250 ml) dry vermouth, and ½ cup (4 fl oz/125 ml) fresh orange juice. Stir in 2 cups (16 fl oz/500 ml) Basic Tomato Sauce (page 24) and the bouquet garni.

Braise in the oven until tender, about 3 hours. Defat the sauce. If the sauce is too thin, whisk in 1 tablespoon tomato paste; if too thick, add more vermouth. Adjust the seasonings and serve right away.

Beef Carbonnade

Dark beer and allspice distinguish this typical Flemish-style braise.

In a small bowl, mix together 1 tablespoon dried tarragon, 1 tablespoon onion powder, ½ teaspoon ground allspice, 1 teaspoon salt, and ½ teaspoon freshly ground pepper. Make a bouquet garni by tying a 4-inch (10-cm) piece celery with leaves, 3 sprigs *each* fresh flat-leaf (Italian) parsley and thyme, and 1 bay leaf in dampened cheesecloth (muslin). Sprinkle 2 lb (1 kg) beef chuck pieces (2-inch/5-cm pieces) with the herb rub and let stand for 30–60 minutes.

Preheat the oven to 325°C (165°F). In a Dutch oven, brown the meat in 2 tablespoons corn oil. Add 2 coarsely chopped yellow onions, 2 coarsely chopped garlic cloves, and 3 peeled and coarsely chopped carrots and sauté until lightly browned, 3–5 minutes. Deglaze the pot with 1½ cups (12 fl oz/375 ml) Roasted Meat Stock (page 20), 1½ cups (12 fl oz/ 375 ml) dark beer, and 2 tablespoons balsamic vinegar. Add the bouquet garni.

Braise in the oven until tender, about 3 hours. Defat the sauce. If too thin, thicken with a slurry of 1½ teaspoons cornstarch (cornflour) mixed into 2 tablespoons water. Bring to a boil and cook until the sauce thickens, about 1 minute. Add more beer if the sauce is too thick. Adjust the seasonings and serve right away.

Red-Cooked Beef

The soy sauce in the braising liquid turns the ingredients in this Asian-style braise an intriguing reddish brown.

In a small bowl, mix together 2 teaspoons five-spice powder and ½ teaspoon freshly ground pepper and season the meat. Instead of a bouquet garni, make a *sachet d'épices* by tying 3 pieces fresh ginger (¼-inch/6-mm pieces), 2 whole star anise, 3 whole cloves, and 1 piece orange peel (4-inch/10-cm piece) in dampened cheesecloth (muslin). Sprinkle 2 lb (1 kg) beef chuck pieces (2-inch/5-cm pieces) with the spice rub and let stand for 30–60 minutes.

Preheat the oven to 325°C (165°F). In a Dutch oven, brown the meat in 2 tablespoons peanut oil. Add 1½ cups (1½ oz/140 g) chopped green (spring) onions (white and pale green parts), and 2 minced garlic cloves and sauté until lightly browned, 3–5 minutes. Deglaze the pot with 1½ cups (12 fl oz/375 ml) Roasted Meat Stock (page 20), ¼ cup (2 fl oz/60 ml) reduced-sodium soy sauce, and ½ cup (4 fl oz/125 ml) Chinese rice wine or dry sherry. Stir in 1 teaspoon sugar and add the *sachet d'épices.*

Braise in the oven until tender, about 3 hours. Defat the sauce. If too thin, thicken with a slurry of 1 tablespoon cornstarch (cornflour) mixed into ¼ cup (2 fl oz/60 ml) water. Bring to a boil and cook until the sauce thickens, about 1 minute. Add more rice wine if the sauce is too thick. Adjust the seasonings, garnish generously with chopped green onions, and serve right away.

Osso Buco

This northern Italian braise, which calls for slowly and gently cooking veal shank until fork tender, is an ideal wintertime dish. *Gremolata*, a classic mixture of garlic, parsley, and lemon zest added at the end, provides a touch of color and brightens the overall flavor of the dish.

1 Make the herb rub and bouquet garni

In a small bowl, mix together the dried sage, salt, and lemon pepper. Set aside. Wrap the sage sprigs, parsley sprigs, lemon zest strips, and bay leaves in a piece of damp cheesecloth (muslin) and secure with kitchen string. Set aside. For more details on making a bouquet garni, turn to page 37.

2 Prepare the meat

To find out more about trimming meat, turn to page 38. Using a rigid boning knife, trim away and discard most of the excess external fat and membrane from the meat. You should keep some of the external fat and membrane intact so the pieces will not fall apart or dry out during cooking.

3 Season the meat

Put the meat in a shallow glass or ceramic dish and coat it on all sides with the herb rub. Cover the dish and let the meat stand at room temperature for at least 30 minutes and up to 1 hour. This gives the meat time to absorb the flavors.

4 Prepare the vegetables

To find out more about preparing the onion and garlic, turn to pages 32 and 33. First, dice the onion: Cut the onion in half lengthwise and peel each half. One at a time, place the onion halves, cut side down, on a cutting board. Alternately, make a series of lengthwise cuts, parallel cuts, and then crosswise cuts to create ¼-inch (6 mm) dice. Be sure to stop just short of the root end; this holds the onion together as you cut. Next, mince the garlic: Place the garlic cloves on a work surface, firmly press against them with the flat side of a chef's knife, and pull away the papery skin. Rock the knife rhythmically over the garlic to mince it. Finally, slice the carrots: Using a vegetable peeler, peel the carrots. Then, using the chef's knife, cut the carrots in half lengthwise and then crosswise into thin half-moons. ›

For the rub

1 teaspoon dried sage

2 teaspoons salt

1 teaspoon lemon pepper

For the bouquet garni

3 sprigs fresh sage

3 sprigs fresh flat-leaf (Italian) parsley

4 lemon zest strips, 2 inches long by ½ wide (5 cm by 12 mm)

2 bay leaves

4–5 lb (2–2.5 kg) veal shank, cut into 2-inch (5-cm) lengths by the butcher

1 large yellow onion

4 cloves garlic

4 carrots

2 tablespoons olive oil

1 cup (8 fl oz/250 ml) dry white wine such as Pinot Grigio

1–2 cups (8–16 fl oz/250–500 ml) Chicken Stock (page 22)

½ cup (4 fl oz/125 g) Roasted Tomato Sauce (page 26)

For the *gremolata*

1 lemon

4 cloves garlic

24 sprigs fresh flat-leaf (Italian) parsley

1 or 2 tablespoons tomato paste

1 teaspoon salt

½ teaspoon freshly ground pepper

MAKES 4 SERVINGS

5>

5 Brown the meat

Position an oven rack in the middle of the oven and preheat to 350°F (180°C). If you need help browning meat, turn to page 37. Place a Dutch oven on the stove top over medium-high heat. When it's hot (you'll be able to feel the heat rising upward when you hold your hand over the pot), add the olive oil and heat until the surface appears to shimmer. Using tongs, add the shank pieces to the pot in a single layer. Do not crowd the pieces or they will steam, rather than brown (you may need to cook them in 2 batches). Cook, turning often, until both sides are golden brown, about 4 minutes on each side. Transfer to a large platter. Pour off and discard all but 2 tablespoons of the fat.

6 Cook the vegetables

Return the pot to medium-high heat and add the onion, garlic, and carrots. Cook, stirring often, until the onion is lightly browned, 3–5 minutes. Browning the vegetables enhances their natural sweetness.

7 Deglaze the pot and add the liquid with the bouquet garni

If you are new to deglazing, turn to page 43. Pour the wine into the pot and bring to a boil, scraping up the browned bits in the pot with a wooden spoon. Stir in 1 cup (8 fl oz/250 ml) of the stock and the tomato sauce and bring to a boil. As soon as you see large bubbles begin to form, remove the pot from the heat. Add the bouquet garni to the pot along with the browned meat and juices from the bowl. The liquid should come three-fourths of the way up the sides of the meat; if it doesn't, supplement it with more stock.

8 Braise the meat

Cover the pot, put it in the oven, and let it cook, undisturbed, in the steady heat of the oven. After 1 hour, use oven mitts to pull the pot carefully from the oven. Uncover the pot and peer into it. If the liquid has evaporated, add additional wine or stock to bring the level back to where you started. Re-cover the pot and continue to braise the veal for 30 minutes longer. >

CHEF'S TIP

Although you can braise beef and veal on the stove top over medium heat, maintaining the liquid at a steady gentle simmer can demand frequent attention. Braising in the even heat of the oven ensures that the meat is cooking at a consistent rate, leaving you free to do other tasks.

9 **Check the meat for doneness**
Place shallow bowls on the stove top to warm from the heat of the oven. After 1½ hours, uncover the pot and insert a fork into the meat; if it slips in and out easily, the meat is done. If it is not ready, re-cover, return to the oven, and continue to cook, testing every 30 minutes. The total braising time is usually 2½–3 hours.

CHEF'S TIP

Gremolata is a traditional garnish for osso buco, but it can be used for other dishes, too, such as soups or seafood stews. Always sprinkle it on food at the end of cooking. Heat releases the natural oils in the lemon, garlic, and parsley, freeing their fresh flavors. If the gremolata is added earlier, the desired freshness will dissipate before serving.

10 **Make the *gremolata***
To find out more about mincing lemon zest, garlic, and parsley, turn to pages 36, 33, and 35. First, mince the lemon zest: With a vegetable peeler, remove just the colored part of the lemon peel, the *zest*. Using a chef's knife, mince enough to measure 2 tablespoons. Next, mince the garlic: Firmly press against the garlic cloves with the flat side of the knife, and pull away the papery skin. Rock the knife rhythmically over the garlic to mince it. Finally, mince the parsley: Pull the leaves from the stems. Rock the knife rhythmically over the leaves to finely mince them. In a small bowl, stir together the parsley, garlic, and lemon zest.

11 **Adjust the consistency and seasonings**
Put the pot on the stove top. Using a slotted spoon, transfer the meat to a plate and cover with aluminum foil. Let the liquid cool for 5 minutes, then use a large metal spoon to skim the fat from the surface. Whisk in the tomato paste over medium heat to create a sauce with a nice, spoon-coating consistency. If too thick, whisk in stock, 2 tablespoons at a time. If too thin, whisk in tomato paste, 1 tablespoon at a time. Stir in the salt and pepper, then taste. If it tastes flat, add salt and pepper until the flavors are to your liking. Remember, the *gremolata* will add more flavor.

12 **Serve the dish**
Return the meat to the sauce and reheat gently over medium heat, 5–10 minutes. Using a large spoon, put 2 or 3 shank pieces with some of the sauce in each warmed bowl. Sprinkle each portion with large pinches of *gremolata*. Serve right away. Pass extra *gremolata* and sauce at the table.

Serving marrow

The marrow found in the center of these veal shanks is considered a delicacy by many. Its rich, meaty flavor is too intense on its own, so it is typically spread on slices of toasted country bread. Fleur de sel, a coarse natural sea salt from the Brittany coast of France, brings out the flavors of the marrow. Diners use specially designed spoons, with long, narrow bowls that slip easily into the hole in the bone, to slide the marrow free.

Scoop out the marrow (top left)
A special marrow spoon, shown here, can be used to remove the marrow easily and cleanly. You can also use a small, sharp knife, like a paring knife, but take extra care to avoid cutting yourself.

Spread the marrow on toast (left)
Lightly toast sliced country-style Italian bread and spread the marrow over the toast. You can also rub each slice of bread with a cut clove of garlic before spreading the marrow.

Sprinkle with salt (above)
Lightly sprinkle each marrow-topped bread slice with coarse sea salt, such as *fleur de sel* or other high-quality sea salt, to heighten the flavors.

Braciole

These small braised beef rolls, popular in southern Italy, reveal a colorful spiral of savory stuffing when sliced. The typical Italian-American filling features fresh, bright herbs, tangy pecorino cheese, and chunks of sausage. The "wrapper" of flank steak becomes meltingly tender when braised.

1 Prepare the meat

Using a chef's knife, cut the meat in half lengthwise, then cut the pieces in half crosswise, to yield 4 equal pieces. Place each piece of steak between 2 pieces of plastic wrap on a stable work surface. Rub a little olive oil on the outside of the top piece of plastic wrap; this prevents the meat pounder from sticking and tearing the meat as you pound. Using a meat pounder or mallet, pound each piece of steak, starting at the center and moving the pounder toward the outer edges, until the meat is an even ⅛–¼ inch (3 mm–6 mm) thick. Do not use too much force or you might tear the meat. Set the wrapped meat pieces aside at room temperature while you prepare the stuffing.

2 Make the bread crumbs

Cut the crust from the bread, tear the slice into large pieces, and place in a blender or food processor. Process until coarse crumbs form.

3 Make the stuffing

Using a rigid boning knife, cut a lengthwise slit through the casing of each sausage, then use your fingers to pull off and discard the casings and break the sausage into small pieces. Put the sausage meat in a cold frying pan and place the pan over medium heat. (Starting the sausages in a cold pan helps them cook more evenly.) Cook the sausage, using a large spoon to break up the meat as it cooks, until no trace of pink remains, 5–7 minutes. Stir in the onion and garlic and cook, stirring occasionally, until the onions are translucent, 3–5 minutes. Remove the pan from the heat and stir in the parsley, 2 tablespoons of the bread crumbs, the sherry, and the cheese. You want the stuffing moist, but not too wet. If it seems too wet, stir in more bread crumbs, 1 tablespoon at a time. If it seems too dry, mix in more sherry, 1 teaspoon at a time, until the mixture looks and feels right. Stir in the salt and pepper, then taste the stuffing. If it tastes bland, add a bit more salt or pepper until the flavoring is to your liking. Set the stuffing aside until cool to the touch, about 5 minutes.

4 Spread the stuffing

Remove the top layer of plastic wrap from the steak pieces. Use a pastry brush to coat each piece of meat on all sides with ½ teaspoon olive oil. Sprinkle the pieces with 2 teaspoons of the salt and 1 teaspoon of the pepper, dividing evenly. Using a spoon, divide the stuffing equally among the 4 pieces of steak. Use the spoon to spread the stuffing evenly across each piece, leaving a ¼-inch (6-mm) border uncovered on the edges. >

---

1 flank steak, about 2 lb (1 kg) and less than 1 inch (2.5 cm) thick

Olive oil for preparing the meat

For the stuffing

1 slice day-old coarse Italian bread

2 hot or sweet Italian sausages, about ½ lb (250 g) total weight

3 tablespoons finely diced yellow onion (page 32)

1 tablespoon minced garlic (page 33)

2 tablespoons chopped fresh flat-leaf (Italian) parsley (page 35)

2 tablespoons Amontillado sherry or Marsala wine

¼ cup (1 oz/30 g) freshly grated *pecorino romano* cheese

1 teaspoon salt

½ teaspoon freshly ground pepper

2½ teaspoons salt

2 teaspoons freshly ground pepper

2–3 cups (16–24 fl oz/500–750 ml) Roasted Tomato Sauce (page 26)

2 tablespoons olive oil, plus 2 teaspoons for brushing the steaks

MAKES 4 SERVINGS

CHEF'S TIP

When a recipe calls for bread crumbs, dried crumbs are usually what is meant. Fresh crumbs contain more moisture than dried and the two will behave differently in recipes, so never substitute one for the other.

5 Roll the beef

Have ready eight 6-inch (15-cm) lengths of kitchen string. Look at the steak and notice which way its fibers are running; this is called the *grain*. Arrange the steak on the work surface so the grain is parallel to the edge of the surface. Use both hands to roll the edge of the steak onto itself, then continue to roll, using the bottom layer of plastic wrap to help you form an even cylinder, enclosing the filling. Remove and discard the plastic wrap. Using the string, tie each cylinder in 2 places, evenly spaced, to hold the cylinder's shape. Sprinkle the exterior of the rolls with the remaining ½ teaspoon salt and 1 teaspoon pepper, dividing evenly.

6 Brown the beef rolls

For more details on browning meat, turn to page 37. Position an oven rack in the middle of the oven and preheat to 350°F (180°C). Put 2 cups (16 fl oz/500 ml) of the tomato sauce into a Dutch oven and put the pot in the oven to heat. Reserve the rest to replenish the braising liquid, if needed. Meanwhile, place a large frying pan on the stove top over medium-high heat. When it is hot (you'll be able to feel the heat rising upward when you hold your hand over the pan), add the 2 tablespoons olive oil and heat until the surface appears to shimmer. Add the beef rolls and cook, turning carefully with tongs, until the entire surface is golden brown, about 5 minutes for each section.

7 Braise the beef rolls

Using oven mitts, remove the Dutch oven from the oven and put it on the stove top. Add the rolls, using a large spoon to push them down into the sauce. The sauce should reach three-fourths of the way up the sides of the beef rolls. If it does not, supplement it with additional tomato sauce. Cover the pot and put it in the oven to braise. When the beef rolls have cooked for 40 minutes, about halfway through the cooking time, carefully uncover the pot and peer into it. If the sauce has evaporated, add additional tomato sauce to bring the level back to where you started. Using tongs, turn the rolls, then re-cover the pot and continue to braise the beef rolls for 35 more minutes. Place individual plates on the stove top to warm from the heat of the oven.

8 Check the beef rolls for doneness

Using oven mitts, remove the Dutch oven from the oven and put it on the stove top. Insert the tip of a small knife into the beef rolls. If it easily slips in and out and you feel little resistance, the meat is done. Braised meat becomes tender at the well-done stage, so you won't need to use a thermometer. If the meat is not ready, re-cover the pot and continue to cook, testing the meat every 5 minutes. The total braising time should be about 1½ hours.

9 Serve the beef rolls

Using tongs, transfer the beef rolls to the warmed plates. Using a knife or kitchen scissors, cut off the kitchen string and discard it. Spoon some of the sauce over the top. Serve right away. Serve the rest of the sauce in a sauceboat.

Rolled Beef Variations

Now that you have learned how to cut and pound pieces of flank steak to an even thinness, wrap them around a stuffing, and tie the resulting beef rolls securely, you have mastered not only the basic techniques for making Braciole (page 125–126), but also several other beef rolls. This trio of variations touches three distinct culinary traditions, German, Italian, and Argentinian. Each one calls for a different stuffing and braising liquid, but all rely on the same steps at the stove: carefully browning the rolls on all sides and then braising them until they are fork-tender and a flavorful sauce has formed. Each variation makes 4 servings.

Rouladen

A piquant coarse mustard pairs well with sour pickles and ham in these German beef rolls.

Cut 1 thin flank steak, about 2 lb (1 kg), into 4 equal pieces and pound them flat.

Next, leaving a 1-inch border, spread ½ cup (4 oz/125 g) German-style coarse-grain mustard on the steak pieces, dividing evenly. Layer ¼ lb (125 g) thinly sliced ham, ½ thinly sliced large yellow onion, and 1 cup (5 oz/155 g) thinly sliced gherkins or other pickles on top of the mustard, again dividing evenly. Sprinkle with 1 tablespoon chopped fresh dill, again dividing evenly. Roll and tie the steaks.

Preheat the oven to 350°F (180°C). In a Dutch oven over medium-high heat, brown the beef rolls in 2 tablespoons olive oil. Transfer to a plate, then deglaze with ½ cup (4 fl oz/125 ml) dark lager. Reduce by half, then stir in 2 cups (16 fl oz/500 ml) Roasted Meat Stock (page 20) and bring to a boil.

Return the beef rolls to the pot, then braise in the oven until tender, about 1½ hours. Defat the sauce and serve the rolls, spooning the sauce over the top.

Rolled Steak with Broccoli Rabe & Pancetta

Salty pancetta is a nice foil for the mildly bitter broccoli rabe in the stuffing.

Cut 1 thin flank steak, about 2 lb (1 kg), into 4 equal pieces and pound them flat.

Next, in a frying pan over medium heat, sauté 4–6 ounces (125–185 g) thinly sliced pancetta until golden, 3–5 minutes. Stir in 2 minced large shallots and 1 tablespoon minced garlic. Increase the heat to medium-high and sauté until translucent, 3–5 minutes. Stir in ½ lb (250 g) coarsely chopped blanched broccoli rabe (page 136) and cook for 2 minutes longer. Divide the stuffing among the steaks. Sprinkle 2 tablespoons toasted pine nuts on top, dividing evenly. Roll and tie the steaks.

Preheat the oven to 350°F (180°C). In a Dutch oven over medium-high heat, brown the beef rolls in 2 tablespoons olive oil. Transfer to a plate, then deglaze with ¼ cup (2 fl oz/60 ml) dry red wine such as Chianti. Reduce by half, then stir in 2 cups (16 fl oz/500 ml) Roasted Meat Stock (page 20) and bring to a boil.

Return the beef rolls to the pot, then braise in the oven until tender, about 1½ hours. Defat the sauce and serve the rolls, spooning the sauce over the top.

Rolled Steak with Vegetables

The inspiration for this dish is *matambre*, a favorite dish of Argentina.

Cut 1 thin flank steak, about 2 lb (1 kg), into 4 equal pieces and pound them flat.

Next, leaving a 1-inch (2.5-cm) border, layer 4 cups (4 oz/125 g) loosely packed spinach leaves on the steak pieces, dividing it evenly. Layer ¼ lb (125 g) thinly sliced prosciutto, 1 peeled and thinly sliced carrot, and 1 thinly sliced yellow onion on top of the spinach, again dividing evenly. Arrange 2 thinly sliced hard-boiled eggs in a row down the center. Roll and tie the steaks.

Preheat the oven to 350°F (180°C). In a Dutch oven over medium-high heat, brown the beef rolls in 2 tablespoons olive oil. Transfer to a plate, then carefully deglaze with ¼ cup (2 fl oz/60 ml) dry sherry or Madeira. Reduce by half, then stir in 2 cups (16 fl oz/500 ml) Roasted Meat Stock (page 20) and bring to a boil.

Return the beef rolls to the pot, then braise in the oven until tender, about 1½ hours. Defat the sauce and serve the rolls, spooning the sauce over the top.

Pot Roast

Like many braised dishes, pot roast is a complete meal, with the meat sliced and served alongside vegetables that have absorbed the rich flavor of the meat during the slow simmer. As the meat braises, the tangy tomato sauce, stock, and hearty red wine gently permeate the beef, ensuring that every slice is rich and juicy.

1 Make the bouquet garni and season the meat

For more details on making bouquet garni, turn to page 37. Wrap the thyme, parsley, celery, and bay leaves in a piece of damp cheesecloth (muslin) and secure with kitchen string. Set aside. In a small bowl, mix together the paprika, garlic powder, *herbes de Provence*, salt, and pepper; set aside. Using a chef's knife, slash through the fat on top of the rolled roast in 3 or 4 places, making sure not to cut the strings. Rub the herb mixture onto the meat until it is evenly coated and put it on a plate. Let stand at room temperature for 30–60 minutes before cooking.

2 Brown the meat and sauté the vegetables

For details on browning meat, turn to page 37. Position a rack in the middle of the oven and preheat to 350°F (180°C). Place a Dutch oven over medium-high heat. When it feels hot, add the olive oil and heat until the surface appears to shimmer. Add the meat and cook, using tongs to turn it, until the entire surface is golden brown, about 4 minutes per section. Transfer the meat to a plate and pour off all but 2 tablespoons of fat in the pot. Add the onion, carrots, celery, and garlic and cook, stirring often, until the onion is beginning to brown, 3–5 minutes.

3 Braise the meat

Add the wine, the tomato sauce, and 1 cup of the stock, stirring well to scrape up the browned bits on the bottom of the pot to *deglaze* it. (For more details on deglazing, turn to page 43.) Bring the liquid to a boil and remove the pot from the heat. Add the bouquet garni and meat to the pot. The liquid should come three-fourths of the way up the sides of the meat. If it doesn't, supplement it with more stock. Cover the pot and put it in the oven to braise. Check the liquid level periodically. After 1½ hours, insert a fork into the meat; if it slips in and out easily, the meat is done. If not, re-cover, return to the oven, and continue to cook, testing the meat every 30 minutes. The total braising time is usually 2½–3 hours. Put a platter on the stove top to warm from the heat of the oven.

4 Finish the sauce and serve the meat

Transfer the meat and vegetables to the warmed platter. Remove and discard the bouquet garni and strings. Let the sauce cool for 5 minutes, then use a metal spoon to skim and discard the fat from the surface. Whisk in the tomato paste. The sauce should have a nice, spoon-coating consistency. If it seems too thick, stir in more stock, 2 tablespoons at a time. If it seems too thin, whisk in more tomato paste, 1 tablespoon at a time. Stir in the Worcestershire sauce, salt, and pepper. Taste the sauce and adjust the seasonings to your liking. Using a chef's knife, slice the meat ½ inch (12 mm) thick. Serve with the sauce and vegetables.

For the bouquet garni

2 sprigs fresh thyme

3 sprigs fresh flat-leaf (Italian) parsley

4-inch (10-cm) piece celery with leaves

2 bay leaves

For the rub

3 tablespoons sweet paprika

2 tablespoons garlic powder

1 tablespoon dried *herbes de Provence* or dried thyme

2 teaspoons salt

1 teaspoon freshly ground pepper

1 boneless beef chuck roast, 4–5 lb (2–2.5 kg), trimmed, rolled, and tied by the butcher

2 tablespoons olive oil

1 large yellow onion, diced (page 32)

2 carrots, peeled and sliced into half-moons

2 stalks celery, sliced

2 cloves garlic, chopped (page 33)

1 cup (8 fl oz/250 ml) dry red wine such as Cabernet Sauvignon

1 cup (8 fl oz/250 ml) Basic Tomato Sauce (page 24) or Roasted Tomato Sauce (page 26)

1–2 cups (8–16 fl oz/250–500 ml) Roasted Meat Stock (page 20)

1 tablespoon tomato paste, or more if needed to thicken the sauce

1 or 2 dashes Worcestershire sauce

1 teaspoon salt

½ teaspoon freshly ground pepper

MAKES 4 SERVINGS

Braised Short Ribs

Short ribs are the meaty ends of the beef ribs and have an intense flavor, here heightened by an initial searing and a fragrant rub of rosemary, paprika, and chili powder. This cut needs long, slow cooking to be tender, and when braised with wine, garlic, tomatoes, and herbs, they have a silky texture and a rich, full taste.

3 lb (1.5 kg) short ribs, cut into serving pieces by the butcher

For the rub

2 tablespoons sweet paprika

2 tablespoons chili powder

2 tablespoons garlic powder

1 tablespoon dried rosemary

1 teaspoon salt

1 teaspoon freshly ground pepper

1 tablespoon olive oil

1 large yellow onion, diced (page 32)

4 carrots, peeled and diced (page 30)

2 stalks celery, diced (page 31)

4 cloves garlic, chopped (page 33)

½ cup (4 fl oz/125 ml) dry red wine such as Syrah

1 cup (8 fl oz/250 ml) Basic Tomato Sauce (page 24) or Roasted Tomato Sauce (page 26)

1–2 cups (8–16 fl oz/250–500 ml) Roasted Meat Stock (page 20)

1 or 2 tablespoons tomato paste, optional

½ teaspoon salt

¼ teaspoon freshly ground pepper

MAKES 4 SERVINGS

CHEF'S TIP
Despite what you may have heard, browning (or searing) meat over high heat does not seal in juices. While it is true that searing creates an appetizing crust on the surface, the only way to ensure your meat is juicy and succulent is not to overcook it.

1 Prepare and season the meat
Using a sharp knife, trim away and discard most of the external fat from the short ribs, leaving about ¼ inch (6 mm). In a small bowl, mix together the paprika, chili powder, garlic powder, rosemary, salt, and pepper. Rub the mixture thoroughly over the ribs, coating them evenly. Put the ribs on a plate and let stand at room temperature for 30–60 minutes before cooking.

2 Brown the meat and sauté the vegetables
For details on browning meat, turn to page 37. Position a rack in the middle of the oven and preheat to 350°F (180°C). Place a Dutch oven over medium-high heat. When it feels hot, add the olive oil and heat until the surface appears to shimmer. Add the short ribs and cook, using tongs to turn them, until they are golden brown on all sides, 8–10 minutes total. Do not crowd the meat or it will steam, rather than brown. (You may need to brown the ribs in 2 batches.) Transfer the ribs to a plate and pour off all but 2 tablespoons of the fat in the pot. Add the onion, carrots, celery, and garlic and cook, stirring often, until the onion is beginning to brown, 3–5 minutes.

3 Braise the meat
Add the wine, stirring well to scrape up any browned bits on the bottom of the pot to *deglaze* it. (For more details on deglazing, turn to page 43.) Add the tomato sauce and 1 cup (8 fl oz/125 ml) of the stock. Return the short ribs to the pot. The liquid should cover the ribs. If it doesn't, add more stock as needed. Cover the pot and put it in the oven to braise. Check the liquid level periodically. After 2 hours, insert a fork into the meat; if it slips in and out easily, the meat is done. If not, re-cover and return to the oven and continue to cook, testing the meat every 15 minutes. The total braising time is usually about 2½ hours.

4 Finish the sauce and adjust the consistency
Put individual bowls on the stove top to warm from the heat of the oven. Transfer the short ribs to a plate and cover with aluminum foil to keep warm. Let the sauce cool for 5 minutes, then use a metal spoon to skim the fat from the surface and discard it. The sauce should have a nice spoon-coating consistency. If it seems too thick, stir in more stock, 2 tablespoons at a time. If it seems too thin, whisk in the tomato paste 1 tablespoon at a time.

5 Season and serve the ribs
Stir in the salt and pepper, taste, and adjust the seasonings to your liking. Divide the short ribs among the warmed bowls and spoon the sauce over the top.

Using Key Tools & Equipment

Fortunately for beginners, the equipment for cooking beef and veal is straightforward. You'll find the pots and pans and other kitchen gear you need to make these dishes will serve you well for all kinds of cooking. The same ample pot you need for stock making is also ideal for boiling a pound of pasta. Measuring tools are necessary for dozens of preparation tasks. And every kitchen needs a basic assortment of sharp, well-balanced cutlery.

Roasting

The best materials for roasting pans are heavy-gauge stainless steel, and anodized or enameled aluminum. The smooth surface of enameled roasting pans are ideal for deglazing and making sauces. It also doesn't scratch as readily as some nonstick pans and makes cleanup quick and easy. A thick and heavy, rather than light and thin, roasting pan is preferable because it conducts heat well and doesn't create hot spots that can cause sauces to scorch. Use a simple rectangular rack for roasting that fits in the pan and doesn't slide around. However, leave out the rack when roasting vegetables along with the meat; you want the vegetables to brown and cook in the fat released by the meat, and a rack tends to get in the way. A roasting pan measuring 9½-by-14-by-2½ inches (24-by-35-by-6 cm) is big enough for a piece of beef or veal weighing about 8 pounds (4 kg).

Sautéing & Stir-frying

There are many sauté pans on the market, and the majority work well. Restaurant-style nonstick frying pans are great for sautéing and pan-searing. These pans, which come in standard diameters ranging from 8–14 inches (20–35 cm), are made of heavy aluminum and coated on the inside with a nonstick surface. They come in a variety of sizes, but the ones you'll use the most are the 10- and 12-inch (25- and 30-cm) pans. One advantage of restaurant-style pans is that their metal handles come with slip-on rubber heat protectors. When you need to finish a steak or small roast in the oven after pan-searing, you can simply slip off the rubber sleeve and put the pan in the

oven. Easy cleanup and maintenance are added pluses. A drawback is the nonstick coating, which can scratch. Always use a plastic spatula and a plastic-coated whisk with these pans. Cast-iron frying pans also can be used for sautéing, although they are heavy and require careful and constant maintenance to prevent rusting. Some cooks like to be able to toss the meat and vegetables by jerking the pan with a snap of the wrist, and cast-iron pans weigh too much to do this.

A wok is the preferred pan for stir-frying, although a large frying pan will also do the job. Many cooks use a standard two-handled rolled-steel wok that measures 14 inches (35 cm) from handle to handle. This size allows them to cook for four to six people at a time, with plenty of room in the pan to stir the food around as it cooks. Woks with a single long handle and nonstick surface are also available, as are flat-bottomed woks for use on electric stoves. Steel woks need regular maintenance. Rinse quickly in hot water and dry thoroughly over high heat to make sure no water remains, and wipe the inside with a paper towel soaked with a little vegetable oil. Wok rings that fit over gas burners help stabilize the pan while cooking.

Grilling

For both charcoal and gas grilling, my two main tools are a long-handled stainless-steel spatula and long spring-loaded stainless-steel tongs (see page 135). The spatula is particularly handy because it allows you to turn steaks or chops without getting uncomfortably close to the hot grill. You will also want a wire or cellulose brush for scraping and cleaning the grate; a buildup of charred food can affect other foods. Aluminum foil pans are useful for indirect grilling to capture the juices.

Braising

A heavy enameled cast-iron Dutch oven is best for braising. Dutch ovens come in a variety of shapes and sizes, but the most popular ones are a 9-inch (23-cm) round pan, a 10-inch (25-cm) round pan, and a 12-inch (30-cm) oval pan. The size and dimensions of the meat to be braised determines what pan you should use. Allow enough space around the meat to allow the air to circulate while the meat is in the oven; 1 or 2 inches (2.5 or 5 cm) should be sufficient. Be sure the braising pan is heavy (so that it conducts heat evenly), is ovenproof, and has a tight-fitting lid. Unenameled cast-iron Dutch ovens, which also come in a variety of sizes, will work well, although they must be maintained to prevent rusting.

Knives & Cutting Boards

I like to use a chef's knife for cutting up or trimming beef and veal: I use 8-inch (20-cm) and 9-inch (23-cm) high-carbon steel knives for most purposes. But both boning knives and paring knives come in handy for trimming.

Wooden boards won't dull your knives as plastic boards do, but they should be thoroughly cleaned with hot water and a chlorine-based cleanser after every use. To avoid cross-contamination (see Food Safety, page 13), use a wooden board for meats and poultry and a separate board for vegetables that are going to be cooked. Lastly, reserve a plastic board for vegetables that are going to be eaten raw.

Carving Tools

Carving steaks and roasts is easy if you have the right equipment. A sharp carving knife or chef's knife is essential. I have carving knives (made from both high-carbon steel and carbon steel) with 8- and 10-inch (20- and 25-cm) blades. You also need a sturdy, long-tined carving fork. A 5- to 6-inch (13- to 15-cm) rigid-blade boning knife is helpful for carving steaks and removing bones from bone-in roasts. Another useful tool is a carving board with a groove around the edge and/or a depression in the middle to catch meat juices, which can be added to sauces.

Mixing Bowls

You can never have too many mixing bowls. The smaller ones can hold prepped ingredients; the largest bowl can be used to mix a salt-dough crust or make an ice bath for chilling stock. Look for tempered-glass bowls that can be used for hot mixtures, too.

Measuring Tools

Ensure accuracy in your cooking with dependable measuring tools. Begin with liquid measuring cups: 1-cup (8–fl oz/250-ml) and 4-cup (1-l) sizes are imperative, and a 2-cup (16–fl oz/ 500-ml) size is handy as well. For flour and other dry ingredients, invest in a nested set of dry measuring cups. For small quantities of spices, herbs, salt, and oils, you'll need a set of measuring spoons.

Puréeing Equipment

When making Yorkshire Puddings (page 47), using a puréeing tool, like a blender or food processor, helps mix and aerate the batter. They're also nice if you like your sauces smooth, rather than chunky. And if you prefer your fresh tomato sauce without skins and seeds, you can pass it through a food mill.

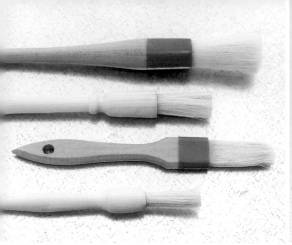

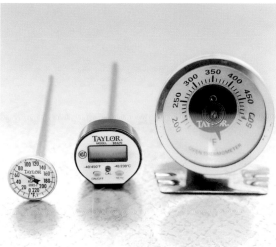
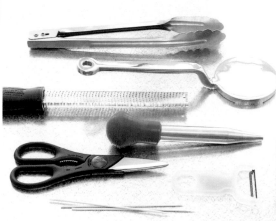

Spoons, Spatulas & Brushes

You'll need a selection of spoons and spatulas for stirring sauce ingredients in pans so they mix together evenly and cook without sticking to the bottom. Use a sturdy, long-handled wooden spoon to stir sauces, and a wooden spoon with a flat bottom or a spatula to get into the corners of frying pans when you deglaze sauces. Heatproof silicone spatulas, which can withstand temperatures up to 500°F (260°C), are good for high-heat cooking and deglazing. Brushes of various sizes are necessary for basting ribs with barbecue sauce and brushing oil onto steaks or pans.

Tools for Making Sauces

Small and medium saucepans come in handy for making sauces. I use heavy aluminum pans lined with stainless steel, but virtually any heavy pan will do. Avoid cast-iron or rolled-steel pans, however, as they will react with acidic ingredients. Stainless steel or plastic whisks are important to have for certain sauces. If you don't have a double boiler, you'll also need a shallow heatproof bowl that rests on the rim of pan to assemble a makeshift double boiler. Finally, you'll find that a fine-mesh sieve is a must for straining clear stocks and sauces.

Bundling Supplies

Cheesecloth (muslin), which can be found in the notions aisle of the supermarket or hardware store, and cotton string are useful when you make stocks. You'll need the cheesecloth and string to bundle herbs for a bouquet garni or *sachet d'epices,* and the cheesecloth for straining solids from stocks.

Thermometers & Linens

An instant-read thermometer quickly and accurately measures the doneness of beef or veal, and a reliable oven thermometer helps you know when your oven is fully preheated and ready.

Equip your kitchen with reliable pot holders, oven mitts, and heavy kitchen towels. They should be thick enough to protect your hands from the heat of steaming liquids and hot ovens.

Other Items

A meat pounder comes in handy when pounding steaks for stuffing. Professional kitchens make frequent use of stainless-steel tongs, and you'll find them helpful when you need to lift chops from a grill or slices of roast beef after carving. Peelers and rasp graters are useful when preparing fruits and vegetables.

Glossary

ALLSPICE The berry of an evergreen tree, allspice tastes like a combination of cinnamon, nutmeg, and cloves.

ARUGULA Also known as rocket, this pleasantly peppery green has sword-shaped, deeply notched leaves usually no more than 2–3 inches (5–7.5 cm) long.

BLACK BEAN SAUCE Made from fermented soybeans, oyster and soy sauce, sesame oil, cornstarch (cornflour), and sugar, this prepared sauce is a popular ingredient in southern Chinese kitchens. It can be found in jars in Asian grocery stores and well-stocked supermarkets.

BLACK TRUFFLE Highly prized underground fungi found primarily in France, black truffles have a strong, earthy aroma that pairs well with beef and veal.

BOK CHOY Also known as Chinese white cabbage, bok choy has long, white stalks with dark green leaves; a mild, chardlike flavor; and a crunchy texture.

BOURBON A slightly sweet whiskey that takes its name from a county in Kentucky, bourbon is distilled primarily from fermented corn.

BROCCOLI RABE Related to turnips and cabbage, this vegetable has slender stalks with small, jagged leaves and florets that resemble tiny heads of broccoli. Broccoli rabe has a mild, pleasantly bitter taste with overtones of sweet mustard. To blanch: Bring the broccoli rabe to a boil in salted water and cook for 1–2 minutes.

CAPERS Capers are the unopened flower buds of bushes native to the Mediterranean. The buds, which are dried, cured, and then usually packed in a vinegar brine, add a pleasant tang to cooked dishes and salads. Capers are also sold packed in salt; rinse them thoroughly before using.

CHEESES
Visiting a good cheese shop is a rewarding experience, since you'll be able to taste the cheeses before you buy. Wrap cheeses in waxed paper or parchment (baking) paper

rather than plastic wrap so they can breathe, and store them in the crisper drawer of the refrigerator, which has the optimum temperature and humidity level.

Gorgonzola A cow's milk blue cheese from Italy with a moist, creamy texture and a complex, pleasantly pungent flavor. When young, labeled *dolcelatte*, it is creamy, soft, and mildly pungent.

Pecorino Romano A pleasantly salty Italian sheep's milk cheese with a grainy texture, *pecorino romano* is primarily used for grating. It has a sharp, pungent flavor and is traditionally called for in recipes that originate in the region surrounding Rome, where the cheese was first made.

CHILES
Chiles range in size from tiny to large, in heat intensity from mild to fiery hot, and in use from seasoning to a vegetable.

Anaheim This fresh chile is long and narrow and can be 6–10 inches (15–25 cm) long. It has a mild taste with a slight bite and is one of the most commonly found chiles in the United States.

Serrano The serrano is similar to the familiar jalapeño in heat intensity and appearance, although it is smaller, usually about 2 inches (5 cm) long, and more slender. It can be green or red.

CHILE POWDER Pure ground chile powder, made from dried and ground chiles, is not the same as chili powder, which is a combination of a variety spices. When selecting pure chile powder, the mildly hot and flavorful ancho chile powder is a versatile choice.

CHILE SAUCE Asian chile sauces come in many colors, flavors, and heat levels. Used as condiments and seasonings, they range from sweet to pungent and are typically made by grinding fresh or dried chiles to a paste with other seasonings. Look for chile sauces in well-stocked supermarkets and Asian groceries.

CHILI POWDER A commercial spice blend that usually combines dried chiles, cumin,

oregano, garlic, cloves, and coriander. It is used to season chili as well as beef dishes that benefit from its distinctive, slightly spicy flavor.

CHINESE RICE WINE Rich amber in color with a full-bodied bouquet, Chinese rice wine is the product of fermenting glutinous rice and millet.

CLOVES Shaped like a small nail with a round head, the almost-black clove is the dried bud of a tropical evergreen tree. Cloves have a strong, sweet flavor with a peppery quality and are available whole or ground.

COCONUT MILK Coconut milk, which is made by soaking grated coconut in water, is sold in cans or frozen in well-stocked grocery stores. It is available in full-fat and reduced-fat forms.

COGNAC This double-distilled French brandy has a full-bodied flavor that pairs well with beef and veal. It is an excellent addition to sauces and braises.

CORIANDER, GROUND Native to the Mediterranean and Asia, coriander is related to the parsley family. It is mildly fragrant and has a flavor akin to a combination of lemon, sage, and caraway.

CORNSTARCH Also called cornflour, cornstarch is used in many sauces for its thickening power. Just a few teaspoonfuls can change a thin liquid into a thick, smooth, shiny sauce.

CUMIN This spice comes from the seeds of a member of the parsley family. It imparts a distinctive aroma and a nutty, smoky flavor when used in rubs for beef or veal.

CURRY PASTE Made throughout Southeast Asia, curry paste usually includes fresh ingredients such as lemongrass, galangal, garlic, onions, green or red chiles, and cilantro. Curry pastes are often classified as green, red, or yellow, depending on ingredients. Indian and Pakistani cooks also make curry paste, but curry powder is more widely used in Indian cooking. Curry paste has a shelf life of 6 months and once opened should be refrigerated for up to 3 months.

FISH SAUCE Called *nuoc mam* in Vietnam and *nam pla* in Thailand, fermented fish sauce is a salty and pungent seasoning used throughout Southeast Asia. It is a common addition to Asian beef dishes.

FIVE-SPICE POWDER Sometimes labeled "Chinese five-spice powder," this potent spice blend varies in its makeup—and often in its number of spices—but usually contains cloves, aniseeds or fennel seeds, star anise, cinnamon, Sichuan peppercorns, and sometimes ginger.

GARLIC When buying garlic, choose plump, firm heads with no brown discolorations. (A tinge of purple is fine, even desirable.) Always take care not to cook garlic beyond a light golden color, or it can taste harsh.

GHERKINS Also called cornichons, these small, tart, crisp pickles are prepared with cucumbers that are specifically grown to be picked while still very small.

GINGER Spicy and sweet in both aroma and flavor, ginger adds a lively note to beef and veal dishes. Hard and knobby, fresh ginger has thin, pale brown skin. Although called a root, it is actually a rhizome, or underground stem. Select ginger that is firm with smooth, unbroken skin.

GREEN PEPPERCORNS Green, black, and white, peppercorns are all the same spice that has been picked at different stages of ripeness and processed differently. Green peppercorns are harvested when still green and unripe. They are then packed in water or brine or dehydrated. They are less pungent than black and white peppercorns.

HERBS
Learning to use fresh herbs is one of the best things you can do to improve your cooking. Dried herbs also have their place; they are ideal for use in dry rubs and in some braises and preparations.

Basil Used in kitchens throughout the Mediterranean, basil adds a highly aromatic, peppery flavor. As basil turns black quickly, be sure to use it soon after chopping.

Bay Elongated gray-green leaves used to flavor sauces and braises, imparting a slightly sweet, citrusy, nutty flavor. Usually sold dried, bay leaves, which are leathery and can have sharp edges, should be removed before serving.

Cilantro Also called fresh coriander or Chinese parsley, cilantro is a pungent herb used extensively in Latin, Asian, and Middle Eastern cuisines. Its aniselike aroma and bright astringent taste are distinctive. Use it sparingly at first until you are familiar with its flavor. When shopping, do not confuse cilantro with flat-leaf (Italian) parsley, which has a similarly shaped leaf.

Dill This herb's fine, feathery leaves have a distinct aromatic flavor.

Fresh vs. dried Use fresh herbs to season pastes, sauces, and marinades. Dried herbs are best in spice rubs, especially if you intend to store them for any time. When substituting fresh herbs for dried, double the amount.

Herbes de Provence A blend of dried herbs, traditionally thyme, summer savory, basil, fennel seeds, and lavender, used in France's Provence region to flavor dishes.

Marjoram A cousin to oregano, this herb has a delicate floral aroma that brings out the deep flavors of beef and veal.

Oregano Also known as wild marjoram, this aromatic, pungent, spicy herb is used fresh and dried for seasoning all kinds of dishes.

Parsley, flat-leaf Also called Italian parsley, this faintly peppery herb is sweeter than the curly types; it adds vibrant color and pleasing flavor to many beef and veal dishes.

Rosemary This woody Mediterranean herb, with leaves like small pine needles, has an assertive flavor that pairs well with beef and veal, but should be used in moderation.

Sage A popular Italian herb with soft, gray-green leaves, sage is pungent and aromatic. Use it fresh and dried in rubs and sauces.

Tarragon With its slender, deep green leaves and elegant, slightly aniselike scent, tender tarragon is a popular addition to meat rubs.

Thyme Tiny green leaves on thin stems, this herb is a mild, all-purpose seasoning. Its floral, earthy flavor complements meats, fish, vegetables, and salads.

HOISIN SAUCE This spicy, slightly sweet, brownish red sauce is made from fermented soybeans flavored with five-spice powder, garlic, and dried chile. It is widely available in bottles and jars in the Asian section of most supermarkets.

LAVENDER, FRESH This purple flowering herb has highly perfumed blossoms, leaves, and stalks that can be used fresh or dried. A signature seasoning of southern France, the blossoms have a sweet and mildly lemony flavor and fragrance and are a component of *herbs de Provence*.

LEMONGRASS An aromatic herb used in Southeast Asia, lemongrass resembles a green (spring) onion in shape. The slender, yellowish stalk has a fresh lemony aroma and flavor. Use only the pale bottom part of the stalk for cooking, removing the tough outer leaves before crushing it with the butt of a knife and then chopping. Since its fibers are tough, lemongrass needs to be minced finely or removed from a dish before serving.

LEMON PEPPER This commercial blend of coarsely ground black pepper and dried lemon zest, lemon pepper is available in most markets. Some spice companies offer blends that also include cumin, oregano, thyme, dried onion and garlic, and/or paprika. You can make your own lemon pepper by mixing coarsely ground pepper with an equal amount of lemon zest.

MADEIRA A fortified wine from Portugal, Madeira ranges in flavor and color from light, nutty, and dry aperitif wines to darker, sweet after-dinner wines. It is added to both savory and sweet dishes, especially rich sauces and braises.

MARSALA A fortified wine from near the Sicilian town of the same name, Marsala is rich tasting, amber colored, and available in sweet and dry forms. It pairs well with both beef and veal dishes.

MOLASSES A thick, robust syrup, molasses is a by-product of cane-sugar refining. It is used in braises, sauces, and marinades and deepens the flavors of beef and veal.

MUSHROOMS

Almost 40,000 varieties of mushrooms exist in the world, but only a fraction of them make it to the table, where they are enjoyed for their rich, earthy flavor. These are some of the more common varieties.

Chanterelle Bright golden yellow and trumpet-shaped, this distinctive wild mushroom is appreciated for its delicate apricot-like flavor.

Common brown Also known as cremini and Italian or Roman mushrooms, these small, cultivated mushrooms mature to become portobellos.

Morel This dark mushroom has a dark, elongated, spongelike cap and a hollow stem. Morels have an intense, musky flavor that pairs well with beef and veal.

Portobello Cultivated mushrooms, portobellos are common brown mushrooms that have been allowed to grow until their caps are about 6 inches (15 cm) wide and dark brown. They have a rich, smoky flavor and meaty texture.

Shiitake The most popular mushrooms in Japan and now widely cultivated throughout the world. Buff to dark brown, fresh shiitakes should have smooth, plump caps.

White Also called button mushroom, this cultivated all-purpose mushroom is readily found in grocery stores.

MUSTARD

At its simplest, prepared mustard is a mixture of ground mustard seeds and water. But this basic paste, available smooth or coarse grained, has been refined around the world by adding flavorful ingredients.

Dijon Originating in Dijon, France, this mustard is made from brown or black seeds, white wine, and herbs. It can be smooth or coarse-grained, depending on whether the seeds are finely ground or left whole.

Dry Mustard seeds come in three colors: white (also called yellow), brown, and black. The white seeds are the mildest, followed in pungency by brown or black. Look for English dry mustard, which is a classic blend of ground white and brown seeds

sometimes mixed with wheat flour for bulk and turmeric for color.

German Mild or hot, hearty, and slightly sweet, German mustard can be coarse or smooth and is typically dark because whole seeds are used.

OIL

Cooking oils, fats that are liquid at room temperature, play an essential role in the kitchen. As a general rule, choose less refined, more flavorful oils for uncooked uses, and refined, less flavorful oils for cooking.

Asian sesame This deep amber–colored oil is pressed from toasted sesame seeds and has a rich, nutty flavor. It is used sparingly as a seasoning.

Chile Asian chile oil, which can vary in heat level and flavor, is made by infusing oil with dried chiles. It is used primarily as a seasoning. Look for chile oils in well-stocked supermarkets and Asian groceries.

Corn Deep golden and relatively flavorless, this all-purpose oil is largely used for general cooking. Using corn oil when cooking beef and veal allows the naturally robust flavors of the meat to shine through.

Olive Olive oil contributes a delicate, fruity flavor to dishes. Deeply flavorful extra-virgin olive oil is used to best advantage in salad dressings or as a seasoning for beef and veal.

Truffle Truffle-infused olive oil, made with black or white truffles, captures the evocative fragrance of the highly prized fungi, with white truffle oil the more strongly scented of the two.

OLIVES

First cultivated in the Mediterranean basin thousands of years ago, olives are one of the oldest and most versatile crops in the world. Olives packed in brine stay plump, smooth, and relatively firm. Salt- or oil-cured olives become slightly dry, wrinkled, and pleasantly bitter in flavor.

Kalamata These olives are the most popular Greek variety. Brine cured and then packed in oil or vinegar, Kalamatas are almond-shaped, purplish black, rich, and meaty.

Niçoise Small, brownish black olives from Provence, Niçoise olives are brine cured and packed in oil, often with lemon and herbs.

ONIONS

These root vegetables, in the same family as leeks and garlic, are some of the most common ingredients. Select relatively unblemished onions that seem heavy for their size.

Green Also known as scallions or spring onions, green onions are the immature shoots of the bulb onion, with a narrow white base that has not yet begun to swell and long, flat green leaves.

Pearl Sweeter than full-sized onions, pearl onions are no more than 1 inch (2.5 cm) in diameter, with papery skins. Because they hold their color and shape well when cooked, they make an attractive visual contrast in a deep brown braise.

Red Also called Italian onion and Bermuda onion, these purplish red onions are mild and slightly sweet. Extended cooking will dull the color slightly but it will also intensify its sweetness. Even sweeter elongated varieties, frequently found in farmers' markets, are called torpedo onions. Grilled or richly caramelized, red onions pair well with beef.

Yellow Yellow globe onions are the common, all-purpose onion sold in supermarkets. They can be globular, flattened, or slightly elongated, with golden skin.

OYSTER SAUCE A thick, dark brown Chinese sauce made from oysters, salt, and water. With its distinctive smoky-sweet flavor, this all-purpose seasoning is used to give body, deep color, and rich flavor to beef sauces and marinades.

PANCETTA This flavorful unsmoked Italian bacon, which derives its name from *pancia,* the Italian word for "belly," has a moist, silky texture. It is made by rubbing a slab of pork belly with a mixture of spices that may include cinnamon, cloves, or juniper berries, then rolling the slab into a tight cylinder and curing it for at least 2 months.

PAPRIKA Made from ground dried red peppers and ranging from orange-red to red, paprika is used dry in rubs, as a seasoning, and as a garnish. The flavor can range from sweet and mild to hot. Sweet paprika is the most commonly used.

PARSNIP A relative of the carrot, this ivory-colored root closely resembles its brighter, more familiar cousin. Parsnips have a slightly sweet flavor and a tough, starchy texture that softens with cooking.

PINE NUTS These small nuts have an elongated, slightly tapered shape and a delicate, resinous flavor.

PORT A full-bodied Portuguese fortified wine, port is available in many types. Ruby and the costlier tawny are two varieties commonly used in beef dishes.

PROSCIUTTO This Italian ham is a seasoned, salt-cured, air-dried rear leg of pork. The best prosciutto comes from the area around Parma, in northern Italy.

SACHET D'EPICES Not unlike a bouquet garni of herbs, a *sachet d'epices* is a combination of aromatic spices tied into a damp piece of cheesecloth (muslin) and used to season braises.

SALT Table salt is usually amended with iodine and with additives that enable it to flow freely. Its fine grain is well suited to dry rubs.

Kosher salt Usually free of additives, this salt has large, coarse flakes that are easy to grasp between fingertips. It is used more liberally than regular table salt or sea salt because it does not taste as salty—you'll need almost twice as much.

Sea salt Available in coarse or fine grains, this salt rarely contains additives and is produced naturally by evaporation. The taste of each variety is influenced by where it was harvested. Sea salt grains are the shape of hollow, flaky pyramids, which dissolve more readily than kosher salt.

SHALLOTS These small members of the onion family look like large cloves of garlic covered with papery bronze or reddish skin. Shallots have white flesh streaked with purple, a crisp texture, and a flavor more

subtle than that of onions. They are often used for flavoring recipes that would be overpowered by the stronger taste of onion.

SHERRY A fortified Spanish wine now made elsewhere, sherry ranges from dry to light, from sweet to heavy, and from pale to deep amber. It is used to flavor sauces and in braising liquids. When selecting sherry, medium-sweet Amontillado is a versatile choice for beef and veal dishes.

SNOW PEAS Also called mangetouts, these flat, wide, bright green peas are eaten pod and all. Choose crisp, vivid green pods concealing tiny peas.

SOY SAUCE This pungent, salty sauce is made from fermented soybeans, wheat, and water. Soy sauce ranges from light and mild to deep, dark, and intense. Reduced-sodium soy sauce, while still high in sodium, has about half the amount of regular soy sauce, allowing the cook more control over the seasoning of a dish.

STAR ANISE A dried star-shaped seedpod of a Chinese evergreen tree related to the magnolia. Slightly more bitter than aniseed, star anise has a distinct, spiced-licorice flavor that complements meat braises. When using whole star anise in a recipe, be sure to remove it before serving.

TOMATO PASTE A dense purée made from slow-cooked tomatoes that have been strained and reduced to a deep red concentrate. It has a low acid and high sugar content and is sold in tubes, tins, and jars.

TOMATOES, PLUM These egg-shaped tomatoes, also known as Roma tomatoes, have meaty, flavorful flesh. For canned plum tomatoes, look for brands low in sodium and other additives. Italian canned varieties often offer the best quality.

TURNIP The common turnip is a root vegetable with crisp white flesh and white skin with a purple cap, although some varieties have yellow flesh and the cap might be green, red, white, or even black. Young turnips are tender and have a mild, sweet flavor. The flavor grows stronger and the flesh woodier with age.

VERMOUTH An Italian fortified wine flavored with various spices, herbs, and fruits, vermouth is available sweet and red, sweet and white, or dry and white. It complements many beef and veal braises.

VINEGARS
Many types of vinegar are available. They can be made from a variety of red or white wines or, like cider vinegar and rice vinegar, from fruits and grains.

Balsamic Aged vinegar made from unfermented grape juice. Balsamic may be aged briefly, for only 1 year, or for as long as 75 years; the vinegar slowly evaporates and grows sweeter and mellower.

Cider A fruit vinegar made from apples and used in many traditional American recipes, including certain barbecue sauces.

Rice Produced from fermented rice and widely used in Asian cuisines, rice vinegar adds a slight acidity to braises and marinades. Look for unseasoned varieties.

Wine This pantry staple is carried in most supermarkets. High-quality red and white varietal wine vinegars are available in specialty-food stores.

WATERCRESS This peppery green has a spicy, clean flavor with rounded, vibrant green leaves.

WHITE TRUFFLE Highly prized underground fungi found in Italy, white truffles have a strong, earthy aroma that pairs well with beef and veal. White truffle is more powerfully scented than black truffle, although its flavor is somewhat milder.

WORCESTERSHIRE SAUCE An intensely flavorful traditional English condiment made from molasses, soy sauce, anchovies, and other ingredients.

ZEST The colored portion of citrus peel, which is rich in flavorful oils. The white portion of the peel, called the pith, should not be used in cooking, as it is very bitter. Pesticides concentrate in the skins of fruits and vegetables, so look for organic fruits when choosing citrus intended for zesting or make sure to scrub well before using.

Index

FREE PRESS

A Division of Simon & Schuster, Inc.
1230 Avenue of the Americas
New York, NY 10020

WILLIAMS-SONOMA

Founder & Vice-Chairman Chuck Williams

WELDON OWEN INC.

Chief Executive Officer John Owen
President and Chief Operating Officer Terry Newell
Chief Financial Officer Christine E. Munson
Vice President International Sales Stuart Laurence
Creative Director Gaye Allen
Publisher Hannah Rahill
Senior Editor Jennifer Newens
Editor Stephanie V. W. Lucianovic
Editorial Assistant Juli Vendzules
Art Director Kyrie Forbes
Designers Marisa Kwek and Adrienne Aquino
Production Director Chris Hemesath
Color Manager Teri Bell
Production and Reprint Coordinator Todd Rechner
Food Stylist William Smith
Prop Stylist Leigh Nöe
Assistant Food Stylist Matthew Vohr
Assistant Food Stylist and Hand Model Brittany Williams
Photographer's Assistant David Turek

PHOTO CREDITS

Mark Thomas, all photography, except the following:
Bill Bettencourt: Pages 33, 36 (ginger sequence),
37 (browning sequence), 57 (left), and 59.
Jeff Kauck: Pages 35 (basil and parsley sequence) and 135 (top right).

THE MASTERING SERIES

Conceived and produced by Weldon Owen Inc.
814 Montgomery Street, San Francisco, CA 94133
Telephone: 415 291 0100 Fax: 415 291 8841

In collaboration with Williams-Sonoma, Inc.
3250 Van Ness Avenue, San Francisco, CA 94109

A WELDON OWEN PRODUCTION
Copyright © 2005 by Weldon Owen Inc. and Williams-Sonoma Inc.

All rights reserved, including the right of reproduction in whole or in part
in any form.

FREE PRESS and colophon are registered trademarks of Simon & Schuster, Inc.

For information regarding special discounts for bulk purchases,
please contact Simon & Schuster Special Sales at 1 800 456 6798 or
business@simonandschuster.com

Set in ITC Berkeley and FF The Sans.

Color separations by Embassy Graphics.
Printed and bound in China by SNP Leefung Printers Limited.

First printed in 2005.

10 9 8 7 6 5 4 3 2 1

Library of Congress Cataloging-in-Publication data is available.

ISBN–13: 978-0-7432-6735-9
ISBN–10: 0-7432-6735-4

ACKNOWLEDGMENTS

Weldon Owen wishes to thank the following people for their
generous support in producing this book: Alison Attenborough,
Jennifer Block Martin, Carrie Bradley, Ken DellaPenta, Marjorie Hrouda,
Emily Jahn, Ashley Johnson, Richard D. Judd, Karen Kemp,
Cynthia Scheer, Sharon Silva, Lindsay Walsh, Kate Washington.

A NOTE ON WEIGHTS AND MEASURES

All recipes include customary U.S. and metric measurements. Metric conversions are based on
a standard developed for these books and have been rounded off. Actual weights may vary.